DON'T TELL!

The Kopriva Family Home, Edgemont, South Dakota

DON'T TELL!

A small town, a big house, no place to hide a family's shame

Emma K. Lee

Bitterroot Mountain
Publishing House

Don't Tell!
A small town, a big house, no place to hide a family's shame
by Emma K. Lee
©Copyright by Emma K. Lee 2026

Interior & Cover Design by: Mark Griswold
Edited by Suzanne Holland M.S.
Photographs: All images in the author's collection

All rights reserved. This book or parts thereof, may not be reproduced in any form without prior written permission, except by a reviewer who may quote brief passages in a review to be printed in magazines, newspapers, or on the web.

Published by: Bitterroot Mountain Publishing House, 2026
For questions or information regarding permission for excerpts, please contact Bitterroot Mountain Publishing House at Editor@BMPHmedia.com

This is a work of nonfiction. Although the author and publisher have made every effort to ensure the accuracy and completeness of the information in this book, we assume no responsibility for error, inaccuracies, omissions, or any inconsistency herein. All slights of people, places, and organizations are unintentional.

This book is intended to encourage, not to diagnose or treat medical, spiritual, or psychological problems. Readers are advised to engage the services of their own physician, pastor, or counselor if they need professional support.

Library of Congress Cataloguing in Publication Data

ISBN: Hardcover
ISBN: Softcover
ISBN: eBook

Printed in the United States of America

10 9 8 7 6 5 4 3 2 1

Though nothing can bring back the hour
Of splendor in the grass,
Of glory in the flower,
We will grieve not, rather find
Strength in what remains behind.

–William Wordsworth
Ode: Intimations of Immortality
from Recollections of Early Childhood

Table of Contents

Introduction

Born in 1943 in a hearse on the South Dakota prairie, I realized early in life that any deviation from what was "normal" was best kept hidden. Good People didn't talk about family problems. The strict Code of Silence of my childhood contained ten commandments that ruled my life for decades:

Put a smile on your face.
Go to church.
Suffer in silence.
Avoid strangers.
Don't ask for help.
Work hard.
Look good.
Be smart.
Pretend all is well.
Don't tell family secrets.

When I couldn't hold my story inside any longer, it began to seep out in journals, poems, and drawings that told more than I ever intended to reveal. My childhood struggles sounded familiar, like traumas my therapy clients were presenting. Perhaps my experience was not unusual after all.

Prologue

When I picked up a lead pencil and a journal at age 11, I never intended to share my thoughts with the world. Maybe I was inspired to "get it all down" by my father, editor and publisher of The Edgemont Tribune, printed in the basement of our home. All I knew was that I felt better after I wrote. And, I had much to tell. Family secrets were too shameful to talk about in a South Dakota town where news traveled faster than my father could print it in the "Locals". My journal was a safe place to hide what I didn't dare talk about.

As a youngster of the 1940's, I inherited Ten Commandments of Proper Deportment: Smile. Look good. Be smart. Work hard. Suffer in silence. Never ask for help. Avoid strangers. Go to church. Pretend all is well. Don't tell what goes on at home.

At 14, I begged God, "Get me out of this place!" Although writing and digging in the garden helped me to work out some troubles, others just wouldn't go away. My twin sister, Emilie, was relentlessly imprisoned by Cerebral Palsy and profound retardation. I became her caregiver from the time I could stand up in my crib. I was a prisoner, too. Mental illness, alcoholism, depression, and abuse were verboten issues, never to be talked about. Although curious townspeople witnessed many of the goings-on in our family, I carefully tucked away in my journal details too shameful to discuss.

Years later, studying French and Abnormal Psychology at the University of South Dakota, I frequently encountered my family in diagnostic case studies. I wasn't ready for my greatest desire, becoming a psychotherapist. First, I had to acknowledge the guilt, shame, and anger that I had buried inside. Until midlife, I settled for a career that felt safe: teaching English and French to normal kids.

As the decades rolled by, I turned to psychotherapists and spiritual directors to explore feelings I had internalized like infusions of poison. Listening to inspiration from Adult Children of Alcoholics directed me with hard-worn wisdom. "We are as sick as our secrets. Take the next indicated step and leave the outcome to God."

Perhaps telling my secrets was not being disloyal to my family. Disclosing my past might help others in the same way Twelve-Steppers encouraged me.

A Master Catechist Certification readied me for church ministry with folks seeking God in hard times. A Marriage and Family Therapist License opened my way to set free the shame-filled and hopeless. As a bereavement counselor, retreat leader, spiritual director, and inspirational speaker, I embraced my own healing. Finally, I felt ready to tell my secrets.

This memoir has presented a mosaic of my family in the big house on Second Street. Emilie was the centerpiece, who bonded us together in care and splintered us with unsatisfied needs. Traumatic events exploded randomly, leaving shards of glass, forming an amazing stained-glass window.

An avid gardener, I trowelled deep into the hard soil of my family plot. "A Gardener's Perspective" at the conclusion of each chapter confirmed that spring follows winter. God has heard the brokenhearted who cry, "Get me out of here!"

God has waited to help all of us, sometimes in unexpected places, like in the secret journal of a young girl.

Chapter One
The Vigil

Saint Luke's Hospital in Aberdeen, South Dakota was the last place I wanted to be on a sultry July in 1983. Yet here I sat, lulled to sleep by the steady rhythm of her breathing, in-and-out, like an accordion bellows. The arms of the overstuffed chair near her bedside seduced me into slumber until a pained shriek jarred me back to duty. In horror, I watched as she tore the binding from her abdomen.

Jolted awake, I reached for the buzzer on her nightstand. The post-op nurse commanded me, "Leave the room right now! I've got to rewrap this surgery site."

Thirty minutes later, I was allowed to return to her bedside. Thanks to pain killers, her moans had been replaced by restful snores. I heard no peace from the voice in my head.

You should have been paying attention, not sleeping! That's what you're here for, to take care of her!

Studying her forty-year-old face, I didn't expect to see a mirror image of myself because we were fraternal twins, not identical. When we were teens, I used to envy her ivory skin, her dark hair, her curvy figure. She looked so unlike the petite, blondish girl I had become.

The portrait painter, Time, had redesigned our faces since I last visited my sister 20 years ago. Her pudgy form under the hospital sheet revealed the sedentary life she'd had. The Redfield School for the Mentally Retarded had been her home since 1961.

When we were infants, Mom turned to our parish priest for guidance.

"What should we do with our retarded daughter? With three other children at home, how can we care for twins when one of them isn't well? We've got no help…what can we do?" Mom implored.

"God has given you this child. You must keep her at home with your family!" the priest replied adamantly.

Looking back, I wanted to scream in rage at that pastor. "It's easy for you to say what *we* should do. You don't live in our house! You don't have to take care of everybody!"

In 1956, Rose Marie Eccher married my dentist brother, Greg. With her expertise as an Army nurse, she surveyed our family with professional eyes. Unlike the parish priest, Rose encouraged our parents to send Emilie away. Rose's advice jarred Mom and Daddy like a high-voltage current. Having a root canal without anesthetic would have been less excruciating for my parents. Down deep, they knew institutionalizing her was the inevitable solution.

Just when my sister was being admitted to Redfield, I was leaving for my freshman year at the University of South Dakota. USD was 425 miles from home, in Vermillion.

Feeling both relief and guilt, I questioned the fairness of my own freedom while my twin sister was locked up.

My mind transported me to childhood, as I observed Emilie sleeping on the hospital bed. The nurse had tied her baby-soft hands to the bedrails. Tears dripped to my shoes, saturating them with pain.

Tragedy had bound my innocent sister since her first breath on Earth! Would I have recognized Emilie in a crowd? Yes,

I could have spotted her anywhere! The gap in place of her left eye, disfigured her permanently.

Returning to the overstuffed chair by her bedside, my mind wandered impulsively to my home in California. My job description there was "Wife and Mom." I had been jerked away from my own family by a call from Rose. Her message stiffened me. "Emilie is scheduled to have a hysterectomy. Could you stay with her in the hospital? You understand her laughter, sobs, and shrieks better than anyone else."

Yes, I could certainly decipher my twin's body language and her two-word vocabulary. For 17 long years, I had been her caregiver while we were growing up.

Rose reported that she had recruited brother Charles to oversee the surgery at Saint Luke's. He was well-qualified for the job since he was a doctor at Yale University Hospital. Unfortunately, Charles could spare only two days away from his medical patients. My assignment was to keep vigil when Charles had to leave.

Keeping bedside watch frustrated me. I hated to waste time and felt restless. Sitting in the hospital with Emilie was boring. My wife and mother role at home defined me as a chauffeur, shopper, laundry maid, and chef. I took time for myself when I taught a faith-formation class at my church. Being in the classroom stimulated me every Tuesday night.

Journaling saw me through many tough times as a kid. Would writing get me through the doldrums at St. Luke's?

Thoughts bubbled up like water from a drinking fountain. All I had to do was push the memory button and emotions spilled out in my notebook.

My second swimming lesson had just begun at the Black Hills Army Depot pool in Igloo, South Dakota. The frustrated swim coach coaxed, "Come on, you can do it! Just jump in. I'm right here to save you."

"I'm scared I'll drown" I whispered in a shaky voice. Paralyzed, I trembled at the pool's edge—eight feet of water only a step away.

With a sudden jolt, I felt two determined hands push me over the edge!

"Sink or swim," was the command I heard right before cold water swallowed me.

My survival instinct triggered a jerky dog paddle. I grasped for the pool edge, stinging water swirling up my nostrils. That day, a nine-year-old learned to hate swimming forever.

My stiff body felt trapped at her bedside in Saint Luke's. Resentment boiled on my emotional stovetop. Unspoken questions shot out like spats of hot oil from an overheated cast iron skillet. I wrote frantically in my journal. "Why must I be the one to sit here? Couldn't a private nurse stay with her? My kids at home needed me."

My mind lurched back to 1953 when she was ten. Her enlarged left pupil looked like it was going to explode. A surgeon had cut the left eye out of her head. Why did she have to be retarded, half-blind and disfigured, too?

Taking another gulp from the fountain of memories, I journaled about the letter I recently found in Daddy's filing cabinet. A medical evaluation written by Dr. Sidney Bailey at the Hot Springs Clinic in April 1944 told the story. The damning report came to my parents when Emilie was eight months old.

"I am very sorry to have to tell you that I do not feel I have anything to offer in the way of treatment for your baby."

Doctor Bailey predicted Emilie would never function beyond a two-year level. The cause of her profound mental retardation had three possible origins:

- abnormal prenatal development
- lack of sufficient oxygen during birth
- brain damage due to Mom's uterine hemorrhage during birthing.

After 40 years, I still felt weighted with self-accusations.

Why was I the lucky one to escape the catastrophe that ruined my sister's life?

Details of our beginnings flowed from my pen. Everyone in my family had a different version of our birth narrative.

Mom went into labor in the wee hours of August 5, 1943. Our hometown could afford only one emergency vehicle. Not an ambulance, but a hearse took Mom to Hot Springs. At three in the morning, we rushed by a Native American encampment named Minnekahta. Out on Highway 18 near the Pringle Cutoff, I was born. A creaky, red water tower marked where the freight train stopped to refill.

Mom told me years later, "Doc feared I was going to bleed to death!"

No one would ever know what really happened in that hearse. What was certain, Emilie was born at four in the morning at Our Lady of Lourdes Hospital. A turning point in all family accounts happened when Mom sank into a coma after Emilie arrived. Mom teetered between life and death for three weeks. At Daddy's insistence, a specialist came from Omaha to save Mom's life by tapping her spine.

According to my brother, Greg (age 13 when the twins came), Mom never regained her mental and emotional equilibrium. The well-organized mother, and President of the Altar Society, became a shadow of her efficient self.

My memories had their own story to tell. Throughout my childhood, Mom complained adamantly about her marriage and her children. In her stress from mothering a retarded child, Mom saw herself as a failure. She feared the wrath of a vengeful God, and she viewed her family as a challenge to her Christian salvation. I heard her rage frequently, and I felt guilty. We were a disappointment to Mom. As a little kid, I thought it was my fault.

If only Emilie and I had never been born....

Mom recounted that I weighed only four pounds six ounces when I arrived. I eagerly gulped infant formula. Emilie could barely swallow goat's milk given to aid her digestion. Quickly, hospital staff noted something was wrong with my twin.

Several months passed before the diagnostic label, Cerebral Palsy with profound retardation, was added to Emilie's medical chart. Dr. Bailey struggled to understand the reason for her condition back in 1944.

I continued to squirm as I sat by Emilie's bedside with my journal in 1983.

Why did God allow such a terrible thing to happen to my twin sister? She never did anything wrong! Why was she retarded and not me?

I was a toddler when Mom introduced me to her friends as *the Well Twin*. That label felt like a curse, not a blessing. I wanted to slither under a rock, out of sight. I didn't want to be compared to Emilie, a retarded child. Feeling both sad and glad was an emotional burden for a little girl to carry.

Daddy, Lawrence Karl Kopriva, held Emilie on the left and Emma on the right. In January 1944, we were five months old and Daddy was 45.

I'd been sitting by Emilie's bed for two days, trying to grope my way out of the fog of memories. I noticed the nurse put padded mittens on her hands to keep her from tearing her incision again.

Some people relaxed with knitting needles twisting in their hands. Others were soothed by a cigarette between their fingers, even when they were not smoking. Emilie self-soothed by shredding whatever she could get in her hands. Mom went crazy when my sister tore her blouse or dropped bits of toilet paper on the floor. Emilie released frustration and boredom by throwing it away.

Huge mittens bound Emilie's hands to the hospital bed, denying one of her few pleasures.

The nurse hadn't noticed the terrycloth scrap I slipped into her palms. Hidden inside her mitten was a secret only the two of us shared. I hoped the rough texture comforted her. Although she couldn't tear it, she could feel it. Perhaps that was enough.

Days and memories passed slowly from my bedside vantage point at Saint Luke's. My anger over being a child caregiver faded. Helplessness wailed a depressive tune.

What could I possibly do to make Emilie's life better? There was no way to rescue her. Sobs overcame me like a flooding river during a winter thaw.

I had better be tough to keep from drowning in this deluge of sorrow.

The gloomy hours passed interminably. Eventually, exhaustion replaced resistance. Serenity came not in questioning, but in accepting. I hadn't *caused* my twin's tragic life. Peace soothed me like a cat's gentle purr.

Nagging questions didn't release their death-grip easily.

What was Emilie's purpose on this planet? What was my role in her life today?

Silence enveloped me, and I burrowed into my armchair, pondering.

On the third day of post-op, nurses stopped at the bedside less frequently. Emilie whimpered softly. I noticed a tear run down her face. She squirmed, telling me to ask the nurse for another dose of pain meds.

Disgusted, I poured out the ice water and the straw a well-meaning candy striper had left. From the nearby sink, I refilled the glass with tepid water.

Emilie didn't drink from a straw, and cold water made her choke. What were you thinking, nurse?

Slowly, my sister sipped from the glass I pressed to her lips. I knew the small gestures that mattered.

My purpose right now was aiding Emilie. That enabled me to feel less helpless.

Little things like adjusting her in a chair, elevating her feet, taking her to the toilet made her more comfortable.

Tonight, she didn't want to eat dinner, not even the cookie I handed her. Reluctantly, she accepted one mouthful of apple sauce before she turned her head away.

When I entered her room on day four, a nurse greeted me with a report. "Emilie is ready for some exercise today. A walk would do her good."

The idea of walking her down the corridor of Saint Luke's caused my palms to sweat.

From long ago, I heard our father's agonized confession, "I would rather take a beating than go out in public with her!" Boy, did I know my father's feeling. Being gaped at by curious onlookers was embarrassing.

Suddenly, I was a fourth grader again at picture day at Edgemont Elementary School. Mom brought Emilie to school for a professional photo of the twins. To my curious classmates, my sister was a carnival anomaly, palsied and drooling. I watched as everyone stared at her. Ashamed of myself for wishing she was not my sister, I couldn't stop feeling self-conscious. I yearned to disappear before the camera recorded my somber grimace and her smiling innocence. With nowhere to hide from the relentless lens, I was captured forever in this agonizing moment.

Fourth Grade Class photo in 1952. Emma (left) and Emilie (right) at age 9.

My mind jumped back into 1983, to our gauntlet walk down Saint Luke's corridor. Folks gawked and turned away when I looked defiantly into their probing eyes. Emilie enjoyed a different experience. She was oblivious to people staring at her. Contented to be moving after four days in bed, she clutched her hospital gown for stability. Onward we went, one step at a time down the hospital hallway. Somehow, I survived our trek amid curious patients and visitors. When we returned to the sanctuary of Emilie's room, the afternoon greeted us with new worries.

Where was Emilie's appetite? Would it ever come back?

Emilie was indifferent to the pudding I pressed into her mouth. She obligingly took a few swallows before banging her fist on the serving cart. If her pounding fist could speak, it would be screaming, "Enough! Leave me alone!" Shocked by her outburst, I moved out of her way until the tempest passed. Whoever thought Emilie couldn't talk didn't know how loudly she communicated when she was mad. I put the spoon down reluctantly.

How different eating had been when we were kids. Mealtime was the highlight of my sister's day. Not bothering with silverware, Emilie would grab a boiled potato from the serving bowl. Shoving it into her mouth, she would hum contentedly as she devoured it. I wanted to puke whenever she did this. Emilie's hands were usually dirty at dinner. Taking care of her was overwhelming, 24 hours a day. When she couldn't wait for someone to help, gobbling was her style.

Today, at Saint Luke's, I would have loved to see Emilie gobble again. She had no interest in food.

Tuesday brought a different story. I wanted to bring out a marching band when Emilie picked up a spoon and began to eat all by herself! She was not humming, but the apple sauce on her breakfast tray had her full attention. I breathed a sigh of relief as she slurped it.

Later, I guided her to the bathroom. "Come on, you can do this."

I remembered when we were kids. When she tried to wipe herself at the toilet, a smeary mess glided everywhere. As I showed her how to turn on the light and flush the toilet, she smiled. She was an eager child who wanted to be a grown-up. My heart wept from stabbing pain.

Later in the afternoon, the doctor made a startling proclamation, "Emilie is going back to Redfield tomorrow."

Did I hear him right? Was my vigil finally over? It seemed like six months, not six days since I left my family in Los Angeles.

In my last moments at Saint Luke's with my sister, I whispered words she would never understand.

"When I'm gone, Emilie, you will forget me as soon as I walk out the door. I won't forget you. I didn't want to come. Now, I'm sad to leave. My voice brings you comfort, like the fabric you hold. You have helped me to accept myself. I don't have to fight destiny anymore. It's okay that I'm the Well Twin."

I raced my tears to the parking lot for the long trip home, grateful to be free at last. Keeping vigil taught me that some destinations were reached only by sitting still. I rested in what was, while letting go of what might have been. Now was my time to move onward.

A Gardener's Perspective

Emilie was a delicate violet with dainty lavender blossoms. She trusted the gentle hands of her gardener. Quiet innocence was her sweet aroma.

Preferring morning coolness to afternoon heat, the violets in my garden grew from four to six inches in height and spread from eight to twelve inches wide. A gentle aura surrounded them in the same way a tender spirit exuded from Emilie. She was content to rest quietly in the present moment without a bit of fanfare.

Chapter Two
Fabric of Life

"Where can I find my sister, Emilie Kopriva?" I asked the receptionist behind the counter in the Administration Building at Redfield State School.

"Give me a minute, and I will look her up. Oh, here she is in Cottage Five, just down the street on your left."

Hurrying down the sidewalk, I was smothered by the South Dakota dry heat. It was July 20, 1985, and my thirty-seven-year-old body was itchy with sweat. Even though I grew up in Edgemont, twelve miles from the Wyoming border, I'd never appreciated the sultry summers of my homeland.

As I entered the lobby of Cottage Five, I spotted her right away. She was the pudgy, middle-aged woman with cropped brown hair, sitting alone on the sofa. Except for the movement of her hands in her lap, she sat still. As I came closer, I noticed the frayed fabric in her baby-soft fingers. Their movement reminded me of Mom's Singer sewing machine that would grasp cloth and guide it forward beneath the presser foot. Absorbed in the moment, she was oblivious to other residents wandering aimlessly about the room.

"Hi, Emilie, it's me, your sister. How you doing, kid?"

She looked up casually, smiling at the sound of my voice. The denim smock she wore was too warm for summer humidity. But the fabric was tough, not easily ripped, and she still liked to rip stuff. Twill shorts and tennis shoes disguised her as an athlete headed out for a run. But her flabby muscles told a different story.

Emilie, locked away in this institution, you are like the fabric you hold, a useless scrap, discarded by society. I want to flee this depressing room full of vacant-faced adults, wandering about in a world all their own. I've travelled all the way from California. How can my visit make one bit of difference in your life?

A flickering smile crossed her face, only to be replaced with a pensive frown. A cloud overshadowed the sunlight of her emotional sky, like smog infiltrating the Los Angeles coastline. What caused the change in her fleeting feelings?

For the first time, I noticed that Cottage Five sang a unique tune. Many voices joined the cacophony, like chirping crickets on an August night. A television across the room blared, but no one paid attention. Amid the clatter, Emilie was in her own sphere. Suddenly, she ripped the fabric she held and tossed it on the floor. Her impetuous movement was a staccato note interjected into the melody of babbling tongues.

"Let's take a walk to the snack bar," I suggested helplessly. "But, first, let's go to the bathroom, so you won't have wet pants," I helped her up and guided her by the arm.

With only one eye, she was like a ship with one rudder. In spite of her limited vision, she moved across the room without bumping into anything. She used the toilet compliantly, without fumbling.

"Can you flush? See, it's right here," I encouraged, pointing to the lever. She did it.

Because she couldn't talk, I assumed she couldn't do much.

Forgive me, Emilie, for not realizing how able you are...you understand more than I give you credit for.

With our parents, we sat on the Burlington Northwest Santa Fe, chugging across verdant Minnesota farmland. It was

September 1948, Emilie and I were five years old. Headed to the Shriners Hospital for Crippled Children in Minnesota, Emilie awaited a new medical evaluation. Our parents were desperate to learn what was wrong with her and what resources were available. The train ride seemed to last forever.

As we passed a small village, Mom tried to soothe our restlessness. She read the city-limit sign, "Look, it's *Sleepy Eye*. What a funny name for a town!"

The locomotive swayed along the endless railroad track, rocking us into slumber. It was nap time for all of us, travelers on a long and solemn search for help.

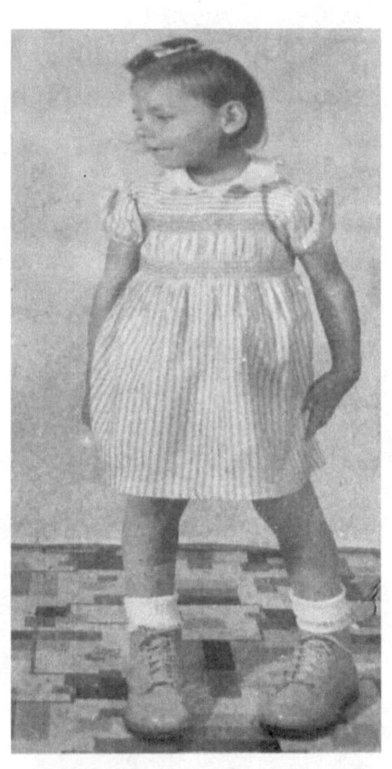

Emilie at age five, when we traveled to Shriners Hospital.

In 1985, I recalled that the doctors at Shriners estimated Emilie would never function beyond the level of a two-year-old. I wondered if they under-estimated her like I had done so many times. When I focused on the things she couldn't do, I overlooked who she really was, a woman able to live in the present moment.

As for me, my 37-year-old brain flooded with concerns of the past and the future. Most of the time, I took this instant for granted, assuming that the present was to be endured until the really important events of life arrive tomorrow. As I observed her, it seemed she had no anxiety about time. Like an ancient sage, she was absorbed only with what happened right now.

The sidewalk to the recreation building seemed familiar to Emilie. She moved confidently in the July heat, like she'd walked that way many times. As soon as we reached our destination, I spied the vending machine in the community room. It boisterously ejected the pack of oatmeal cookies that I chose for Emilie. She devoured them with no concern for the crumbs gathering on her face and scattering on her smock. She hummed contentedly, while my memory camera clicked the moment, capturing the sweetness of life, blended with the tartness of tragedy. Sugar and salt seasoned the cookie recipe.

Life was a combination of joy and pain, mixed like a batch of cookie dough.

Slowly making our way back to her room, I heard my choked voice, "I must go home now, Emilie. I pray that God will take care of you until I see you again."

I watched her settle into a familiar spot on the sofa. When she looked comfortable, I rushed through the front door of Cottage Five to escape sadness and return to a world where there was no room for frayed fabric or fumbling fingers.

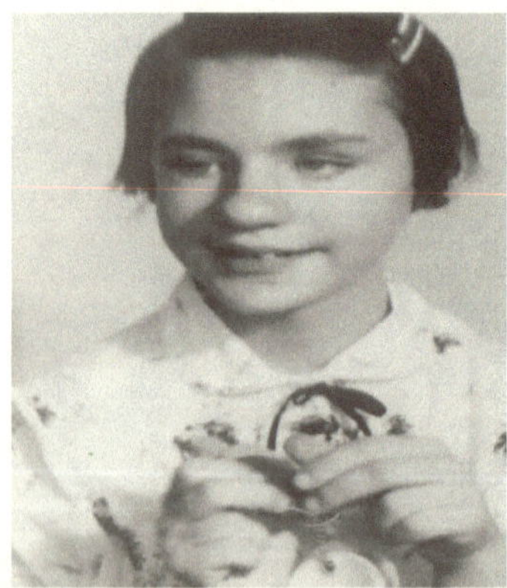

When Emilie was 12 years old, Mom had a hard time keeping her glass eye sterile and in her head. The toys Mom gave her to hold did little to distract her from tearing her clothes.

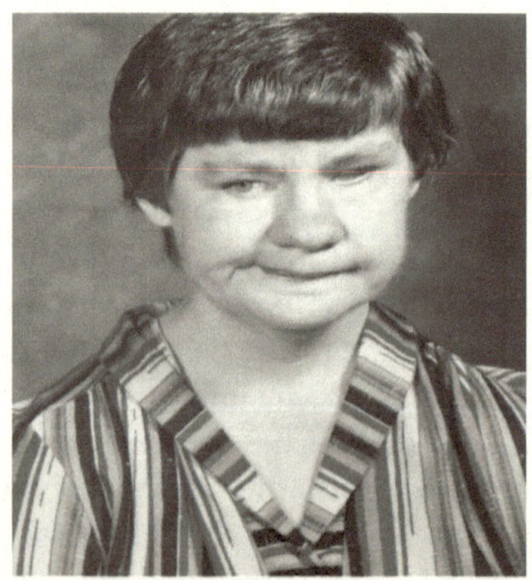

By 1984, Emilie was 41. She had lived at Redfield for 23 years. Her glass eye had been missing for a long time

A Gardener's Perspective

Tall Cottonwood trees surrounded the Kopriva house in Edgemont, South Dakota. In the summer, their seeds floated silently to the ground and carpeted the lawn like fluffy bits of cotton candy. While Emilie found no interest in toys, she enjoyed pulling fabric to pieces and watching it float to the floor like the puffy seeds. Her busy fingers frayed the collars and pockets of her cotton shirts, stimulating her humdrum world.

Chapter Three
The Well Twin

There were no secrets in a small town, where gossip traveled like a wildfire in a windstorm. Soon after my sister and I were born in 1943, everyone knew that one of the Kopriva twins was "not right." Mom faced the situation head-on when she introduced me to friends.

"This is Emma Katherine, the Well Twin," she proclaimed matter-of-factly. An impressionable toddler under a microscope, I was stuck with a label far more enduring than a Post-it note. Standing beside me, Emilie passively held Mom's hand and stared nonchalantly into space, unaware of the power of names.

How dare I be well when my twin sister was not?

Years flowed like a rushing stream. In 1956, Rose Eccher married our big brother, Greg. She observed, with the professional eye of a registered nurse, that our entire family needed help. We were doing our best to care for Emilie, but it felt like we were on duty in an emergency room 24/7. As I watched through the frightened eyes of a thirteen-year-old, I knew we were different from other families.

Our older sister, Bernie, had been hospitalized in Denver for depression by the time she was twenty-two. Our distraught mother, when she wasn't dissociating, was prone to outbursts of rage. Our father's drinking led to afternoon blackouts on the sofa.

Yes, Rose got the picture right…our family was going downhill as fast as a sled on a snowy mountain.

Terrified by frequent arguments exploding at our dinner table like shotgun shells, I discovered there was nowhere safe to go except into myself. I shut down. I shut up. I hid like a soldier in a trench, trying to survive on a battlefield of desperation.

Doctor Leeds, the pediatrician in Hot Springs, South Dakota, had advised our parents to let go of Emilie and focus on the four other kids in the family. It took 17 years of battling guilt and grief before Mom and Daddy institutionalized my twin sister. Daddy was 62 years old, and Mom was 57. Failing health finally forced them to follow Dr. Lead's advice given so many years before.

With the paperwork for Emilie's admission to Redfield State Hospital completed, her departure from our home became imminent. Weighed with a ton of sorrow, Mom painstakingly packed my sister's clothes. As I watched from a distance, not knowing how to comfort my mother, she deliberated about which toys to send along to the institution.

The February morning in 1961, when Emilie was taken away from our family, felt like a funeral scene—the part where the casket was hoisted into the hearse. Instead of a funeral director, the County Sheriff appeared on our doorstep that winter day. He assisted Emilie into the sedan that would take her 365 miles from the only home she had ever known. Deep inside, we all knew that she would never come home again!

As she eased into the backseat of the sheriff's car, my sister contentedly threaded a swatch of fabric through her fingers. My parents and I watched silently, frozen in grief like the rigid icicles gripping our rooftop.

It felt like curious neighbors were gaping at us through their curtained windows, watching the drama playing out in front of the Kopriva place. The driver slowly crawled down Second Ave. toward Hwy. 18, out of town.

Questions didn't wait until Emilie was out of sight before they began pounding me, the only kid left at home.

Who am I since I'm no longer Emilie's caregiver? Will I still be Mom's housekeeper? Will Daddy finally see me?

For certain, I knew who I was not! I wasn't my mother, even though I carried her name. Baptized *Emma*, I insisted on going by *Emmy*. I didn't want to be like Mom, who was always lost in thoughts. She seemed disgruntled by unfulfilled dreams of what her family should be, but never would be. Mom's unpredictable explosions of rage had always made me jumpy. I wanted desperately to please her, but Emilie had always been her priority. All my life, I felt like an indentured servant, earning my board and keep by cleaning the house and looking after my sister.

Now that Emilie was gone, my parents scrutinized me like a lab specimen. I squirmed at being the center of attention. I had nothing to talk about with them. Invisible for years, I was used to being a wallpaper child, just part of the background when family drama unfolded.

Our quiet house was unsettling. I wanted to hide.

Who was this Well Twin apart from her unwell sister?

My search for a self-image was not a new quest. It began when I started Edgemont High School in 1957. I decided to buckle down and be a good student. I wanted to prove to myself that I wasn't "slow" or "dull" like my twin. Following the Kopriva Standard of Academic Excellence, as my two older brothers did, provided me with direction. To my amazement, studying Greek and Roman myths in Latin class stirred up philosophical questions. Was I tough, like the Greek Goddess Athena? Or was I a homebody like Hestia? Gods and goddesses of classical mythology always seemed to be at war, just like my family.

Why was the world a battle ground full of conflict and struggle?

Even though I felt proud when my name appeared on the school honor roll, the critical voice in my head chastised. "No matter how much you achieve, you will never be as bright as your brothers." The gender-bias that women were not as smart as men matched the family expectation that I would never amount to much. Although I wanted to hide in ordinariness, I did desire to be noticed, too.

I doubled down on my studies, locking myself in our small bathroom to do my homework on cold winter nights. The downstairs furnace kept me warmer than I felt in my second-floor bedroom. Studying gave me an excuse to isolate from my parents. “A Good Student”—that was who I was.

In May of 1961, Daddy crowded himself into my world, offering to help me practice the valedictory speech I’d written for high school graduation. Communicating clearly was Daddy’s specialty. After all, he had over forty years of experience as a newspaper editor and publisher. “Speak slowly. Project your voice,” he urged me from the far side of the printshop where he critiqued my presentation. I had Daddy’s full attention at last, but being in his spotlight made me squirm. He wanted me to make a “good showing” because I was a Kopriva. He was proud that I was a hustler, a hard worker like he was.

How could I trust my father who had seldom acknowledged me?

How could I let him into my life after seventeen years of being invisible? My job had been to help Mom upstairs, cleaning house and tending Emilie. My siblings had Daddy’s full attention by helping him print the newspaper in the basement. To me, my father was a stranger.

Although I was grateful for his interest in my valedictory speech, I felt awkward being alone with him when I rehearsed. My “Farewell, but Not Goodbye” talk reflected the conflict within me. I wanted to escape from my family and yet, I wanted to be connected.

I never spoke in public without thinking of him, a father who tried to love me, but didn’t know how to reach me after so many years of not connecting.

Academic achievement meant more to me than just a way of getting attention. Good grades proved to the world that I was normal. My twin sister may have been mentally retarded, my older sister may have been mentally ill, and my mother may have been emotionally distraught, but I was none of those things.

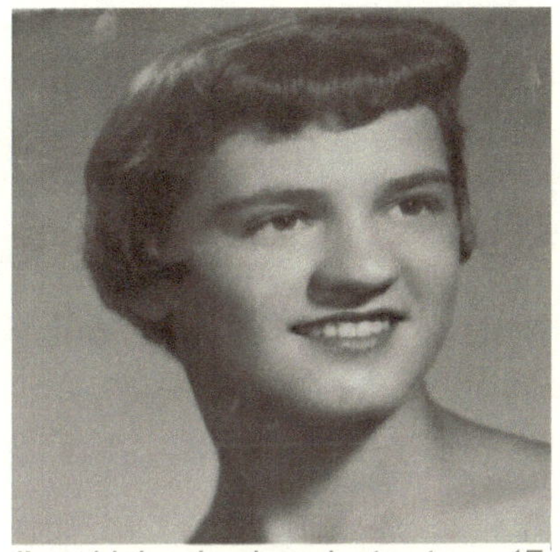

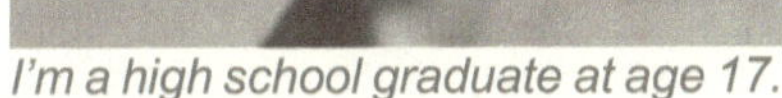

I'm a high school graduate at age 17.

Daddy at his desk in the Tribune office.

Good grades and perfectionism compensated for the shame I felt about the mental illness in our family My two brothers were achievers to the core. Greg, thirteen years older than I was, recalled that in his teens, he decided to be outstanding. After he finished Creighton Dental School in 1956, his patients displayed sparkling grins.

Brother Charles, just three years older than I was, became head of the Department of Anesthesiology at Yale. That followed medical school at Harvard. The three of us Kopriva kids set out to prove to ourselves and to the world that we were not tarnished by mental illness.

What about my sister, Angela Bernadette? She was not an achiever but a casualty. Bernie, a vulnerable 11-year-old when her little sisters were born, watched her world crumble. Mom lapsed into a coma for three weeks and almost died soon after birthing twins. Bernie's world was turned upside down, and it never turned upright again through 90 years of living. She was institutionalized in a mental hospital six times. Meanwhile, Emilie was diagnosed with Cerebral Palsy and profound retardation.

A helpless bystander, I cried out, "God, what is the meaning of this?"

God replied, "It is not yours to know."

I continued to ponder.

What is the Well Twin to do with her life? Is she outstanding in any way? Are women made only for caregiving: teaching, nursing, and motherhood? Will I be exceptional like my older brothers? Or will I always be a lackluster little sister?

Questions buzzed in my head like bees in a hive.

Concealed even from myself, latent anger was a bombshell, lying dormant on the battlefield of my subconscious. It was waiting to ignite when I was strong enough to bear the shock.

At five-years-old, my stuffed toys made well-behaved students, captivated by whatever I wished to teach them. Playing school was fun for me, but not for Emilie. No matter how hard I tried to get her attention, she wandered without purpose around the room. I needed to let go of my expectations of her. She was just like the stuffed toys I instructed, mute and unresponsive. Despite my sister's inability to focus, my classroom proceeded, day by day, enlivened with my undeterred enthusiasm for teaching what I knew.

When I learned to read, I found Mom's Nebraska Teacher's Manual of 1924. She had taught at the country school in Wood Lake. My fourth-grade teacher gave me permission to read aloud poems of Thanksgiving turkeys and Christmas shepherds. When I read to my classmates, the timid child I was at home vanished amid rhyming words and repetitive alliteration.

In my teenage years, while my high school peers were hanging out at the soda shop after school, I was home washing the dishes Mom had stacked in the kitchen sink. Socially awkward, I had few friends and no dates. I withdrew to the safety of my own company at home. Doing chores provided a way to avoid loneliness.

At age 20, my mother, Emma Stasch, waited at the train station to get home to her parents' farm in Nenzel after a week of teaching. She taught at four prairie schools prior to marrying my father in 1929. I inherited her fondness for the classroom.

Looking back on early years in Edgemont, I realized my parents tried to help me to be a normal kid. When I turned 11, Daddy bought an old, out-of-tune piano. Mrs. Bell, a local rancher's wife, showed up each week to oversee my music lessons. Soon Elvis Presley captured my innocent heart when I passionately played, "Love Me Tender". Music drew me to the keyboard often. Practicing my lessons was not a task, but an escape into a happier world.

Mr. Hatton, Director of the Edgemont High Band, invited me to play *the bells*. The heavy xylophone was a burden because I was petite, weighing 100 pounds. Being part of the Friday night football half-time show delighted me.

The school drama program enticed me to perform in one-acts. Taking on the role of an imaginary character was a break from the caretaker role I knew at home. I enjoyed being part of the cast, struggling with my lines.

September 1961, I headed for the University of South Dakota in Vermillion, 425 miles away. Burgess Hall became my new residence. Most freshmen made an exodus for home every weekend, leaving me in a stone-silent dorm.

Could I possibly be homesick for the family I desperately wanted to leave behind?

As my studies progressed, I found Abnormal Psychology intriguing. Recognizing my own family in case studies was troubling. I wanted to forget the mess I left behind. French and English were less threatening to my peace-of-mind than Psychology. Being in the classroom felt safer than working in a mental health clinic.

A Bachelor of Arts Degree prepared me to teach in Wyoming and Colorado in the 1960's. I was not emotionally ready for the career that enticed me, psychotherapy. A Master's Degree in Counseling Psychology from Mount Saint Mary's College in Los Angeles followed in 1990.

In 1995, The Board of Behavioral Sciences granted me a license to do the work that life had prepared for me. I served as a private school counselor for17 years and a psychotherapist for 22 years. Teaching adults basic Catholicism for 27 years drew me to the classroom and closer to God.

My childhood showed me far more about helping people than any academic program ever did. It took decades to accept myself and to trust in the adventure of every season.

A Gardener's Perspective

In an era of gender confusion, a question arose that prior generations didn't ask. "How do I self-identify?" When I attempted to describe myself, I saw a dandelion, a hollyhock, or a sunflower. Choosing only one of these strong yet fragile beauties seemed impossible. I thumbed through an old journal until I stumbled upon a poem I had written in 1988. That made my decision clear.

Don't Tell!

Just A Little Flower

Saint Therese, on your Little Way,
You hear us when we come to pray.
As a sign of tender love,
You send a rose.

For a rose, I do not ask.
I have for you another task.
In God's Garden, let me be
A lovely rose.

My child, know beyond a doubt,
In God's sight and mind and heart,
You've been and will always be
A precious rose.

I was a rose, producing blossoms while protecting solitude, ephemeral yet enduring. Being an encouragement to others during dry, thorny seasons was my way to honor the Master Gardener.

Chapter Four
Bernie's Dance

I became an expert in survivor guilt and secondhand grief as I observed my two sisters struggle through life. That I hadn't caused their pain brought me no comfort. Jagged sobs, like shards of breaking glass, exploded from my throat as I wrote. To my surprise, when I shut off my computer, I felt exhilarated, not defeated. The enduring spirit of Bernie strengthened me. Acknowledging my sadness released joy. As a little kid, I hadn't yet seen the connection between emotions. All I knew was that I hurt.

When I thought about my big sister, my mind flew to 1951. Bernie was 18 years old and fresh out of high school.

Our family doctor dropped a bombshell. "Something's wrong with Bernie. She needs to get away from home."

Mom and Daddy enlisted our brother, Greg, to drive Bernie to Bowbells, North Dakota for a vacation. Spending the summer with cousins on their farm was a temporary fix that lifted Bernie's depression. By September, she was ready to tackle a secretarial program at Saint Mary's College in Omaha, Nebraska. Greg, a student at Creighton Dental School, was close enough to keep an eye on her.

College life went smoothly for Bernie until the day she got an urgent phone call from Daddy.

"My assistant printer at the Tribune just told me he's quitting. I can't possibly publish the newspaper by myself. You must get home right away to help me!"

I was a sixth grader when Bernie returned to Edgemont. From the shadows, I solemnly observed my sister's life shrink into the walls of our basement print shop. Daddy paid Bernie a modest wage, and he provided her food and lodging. But her soul now belonged to the family business, giving her little time to call her own. With few friends her age in our small community, Bernie's daily schedule became a case study in drudgery.

Bernie asked permission to use the family car to meet friends at a coffee shop after work.

Reaching in his pocket for keys, Daddy replied, "Here, take the Dodge."

Mom screamed, "Stay home. You shouldn't be running around all hours of the night!"

A ten-minute blow up finally subsided when Daddy handed Bernie the car keys.

Withdrawing like a whipped puppy, Bernie whispered, "Well, if it's going to cause this much trouble, I guess I'll just stay home."

My sister softly closed her bedroom door. The house was quiet at last. Mom had won the battle, and we all lost the war. Bernie, a casualty of the skirmish, covered herself with a well-worn blanket of depression and dozed off to sleep. Tomorrow would be a repetition of the same tragedy.

A helpless spectator of the conflict, I wished to vanish. I had no safe place to go. My voice was silent, but my heart was sobbing for Bernie. I didn't want to add to the fray. I became as invisible as a virus floating in the air.

My silent partner, Emilie, and I witnessed every family fight. Bernie wasn't the only girl fighting for her life in our household. Emilie had her own issues. The pupil of her left eye had grossly enlarged. Our family doctor quickly referred Emilie to an ophthalmologist in Rapid City. Soon, a hard glass eye stopped up the hole where a beautiful blue eye used to be.

Amid this windstorm of health issues, Mom was recovering from surgery to uplift female organs sagging since she gave birth to twins.

Meanwhile, Daddy kept plugging away in the basement. The Edgemont Tribune continued to appear in mailboxes every Wednesday. A swig or two of Jack Daniel's quelled his gnawing anxiety and hopelessness.

We all did our best to keep functioning, like soldiers marching to the same old drill. By 1954, Bernie, imprisoned in the basement print shop, couldn't continue the routine. Our hometown doctor decided to institutionalize her for the first time.

On August 30, 1954, Bernie received her first electro-stimulation treatment at the hands of Dr. Franklin Ebaugh, Director of the Colorado Psychopathic Hospital in Denver. Shock treatments were the protocol of the day in cases of depression. Loss of memory was a common side effect of EST. At age 22, Bernie was much too young to be losing her memory! Doctor Ebaugh reported that Bernie was depressed, not psychotic. She was to be released from the hospital in two weeks if she responded well to treatment.

As this drama unfolded, our brother Charles, age 14, starting his first year in high school. Emilie and I were 11 and helpless bystanders to an unending nightmare.

This was not the last series of EST Bernie would endure. She received about fifty treatments at Yankton State Hospital, in South Dakota where she was an inpatient five times between 1954 and 1964.

I completed my undergraduate studies at the University of South Dakota. Bernie was just twenty-six miles down the highway from USD.

I hung out with the Newman Club, a Catholic social group at USD that participated in charitable community projects. Once, I tagged along with students going to Yankton to visit lonely mental patients. I told no one that my big sister was locked away at that very institution.

Family secrets were safe with me!

Soon after we arrived at the hospital, I slipped away from the group, looking for Bernie. How unsettled I felt when I saw dazed, drugged patients wandering around the wards. My own sister was somewhere in this house of horrors. I felt obligated to find her, but I feared what I would encounter.

I don't remember if I ever connected with Bernie that day. Certainly, I never returned to visit again. Sixty years later, guilt still weighed like a chain around my neck.

During an interval when Bernie was not in the hospital, she enrolled at Chadron State College in Nebraska. She stayed for only a month before dropping out. She worked at restaurants as a dishwasher or waitress. Holding a job was difficult for Bernie. When she saved enough money, she purchased a yellow second-hand convertible. Soon, road trips across the country with boyfriends added a spark to her dreary life. Anywhere from Vermont to Utah became her destination.

Bernie's sojourns followed a pattern. She would take off without telling anyone in the family where she was headed. When she became destitute, she would phone. home. Sometimes, law enforcement or concerned bystanders called us to help her. Greg, being the elder son, and his wife, Rose would hop on a plane and bring her home.

During the ten-year period of Bernie's cross-country forays, I was between 11 and 21 years old. Once, Rose sent me on a Greyhound Bus to Kemmerer, Wyoming to check up on my big sister. I found Bernie living in a basement apartment and working a minimum-wage job. Troubled by worries, she spent the night pacing the floor. When I got back home, I reported with a heavy heart to Rose, "Bernie is getting by, but just barely."

The most troubling road trip Bernie made during her escapade era took her to Salt Lake City. There a criminal held her prisoner at knifepoint in his apartment for several weeks. My sister was forced to eat scraps from the restaurant where her captor worked. He knew Bernie's history of hospitalizations. He threatened to send Bernie to a mental institution if she tried to escape from him. Neighbors called the police when they overheard violent fights.

Greg and Rose rescued Bernie once more. Soon her shock treatments resumed at Yankton.

In the Fall of 1964, Bernie escaped from Yankton during visiting hours! She simply walked away from the facility with a friend who had a car. After two months of nationwide searching, law enforcement found her in Marshall, Minnesota. My sister earned a living by babysitting, housecleaning, and pulling guts at Swanson's Turkey Plant.

Since a generous widow cared for her daily, Bernie's doctors decided she was ready to live independently.

In 2007, I decided to visit my sister in Marshall. One afternoon, she carefully removed a crumpled letter from her wallet. To me, it looked like an insignificant, tattered scrap of paper. To my sister it was her Bill of Rights. The Discharge document, written by Doctor Behen, Superintendent of Yankton Hospital, certified Bernie was of sound mind,

"Wow, Bernie, I'm so proud of you!" I exclaimed.

She beamed. "No one will ever lock me up again!"

This certificate was her most prized possession that she always carried with her. She worried about losing it. I made several copies for her at a nearby drug store, and I kept one for myself.

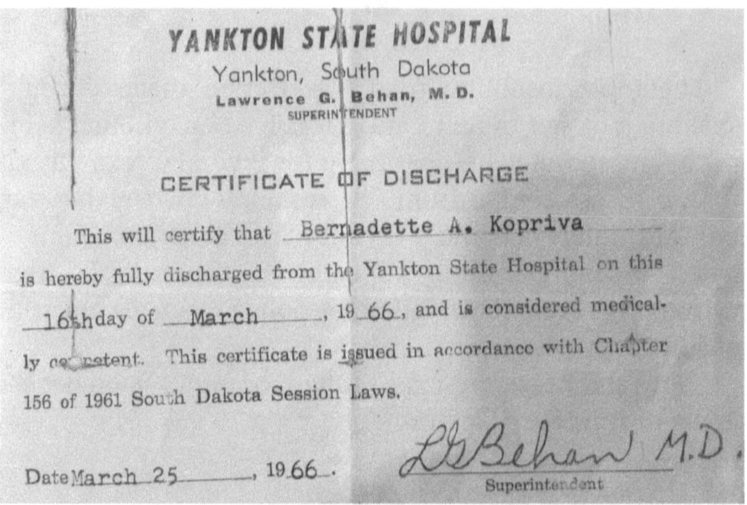

YANKTON STATE HOSPITAL
Yankton, South Dakota
Lawrence G. Behan, M. D.
SUPERINTENDENT

CERTIFICATE OF DISCHARGE

This will certify that Bernadette A. Kopriva is hereby fully discharged from the Yankton State Hospital on this 16th day of March, 19 66, and is considered medically competent. This certificate is issued in accordance with Chapter 156 of 1961 South Dakota Session Laws.

Date March 25, 19 66.

LGBehan M.D.
Superintendent

One creased scrap of paper officially set my sister free from mental institutions forever.

Through the years, family members helped Bernie in whatever way we could. Brother Charles filled out the application for Social Security Disability for her. Low-income housing, and Minnesota health benefits provided her basic needs.

Although Bernie was no longer hospitalized, the scars of mental illness were raw. Sustaining friendships was an ordeal. Her conversations often ended in arguments. Gathering with more than one person at a time, my sister defended one and criticized the other. She was unable to participate in normal social exchange. Male companions were either old enough to be her father or young enough to be her son. She never married. She was quick to label any male acquaintance a boyfriend.

A caring woman from church or a taxi driver took Bernie to Walmart or Shopko for household purchases. Bernie had relinquished her driver's license years ago because she couldn't focus on the road. Occasionally, a boyfriend drove Bernie to Redfield State Hospital, a 160-mile trip. Photos from 1974,1978, and 1992 revealed Bernie with her retarded sister, whom she labeled, "The Poor Little Kid".

Bernie (age 46) visited Emilie (age 35) in 1978.

I visited Bernie every few years. Her unpredictable, hurtful remarks made me shrivel up and stay alert for criticism when I was in her presence.

Did my sister resent me because I had a marriage and a career?

Discussing our childhood in Edgemont was a safe topic that we enjoyed. Bygone days evoked common ground rather than a battlefield. I felt relieved when we chatted without a blow up. A favorite memory from the 1950's always made Bernie and me smile.

We were at home in Edgemont one afternoon when a Country Western ballad blared from the Philco in our living room. Bernie couldn't resist a catchy tune. Impulsively, she grabbed Emilie and began to gyrate to the rhythm.

Emilie shrieked wildly with laughter.

"What's going on?" Mom yelled worriedly from the kitchen.

Daddy gazed in delight; a smile stretched across his tired face.

From the sidelines, I timidly watched the shenanigans explode.

For an unforgettable moment, we were one, happy family. . .all cares were cast aside.

Through the years, Bernie softened when she spoke of Emilie. My two sisters had a connection all their own.

My niece, Mary, and I dropped in at Prairie View for a surprise visit with Bernie in 2022. We drove all day after leaving a family Memorial Day gathering in Rapid City. Bernie, seated alone in the dining room, asked in surprise, "Who are you?" Then recognition lighted her face with sunshine.

I replied, "We just stopped in this evening to let you know we are in town. We will be back tomorrow to spend the whole day with you."

The next morning, Mary and I arrived at Prairie View in time for a worship service. Bernie can't follow the hymns in the song book, and the preaching seemed way over her head.

"It's good you came. It shows folks here that somebody cares about me," Bernie stated matter-of-factly.

When she unwrapped our gifts, Bernie said, "It feels like Christmas!"

Our voices chimed excitedly, "It's time for a party!".

I put Patsy Cline on the CD player and turned up the volume. Without delay, we each did our own dance moves. Seated in the wheelchair, Bernie wiggled and giggled to the beat. "This is so fun!" Bernie shouted above the din. Mary and I were decked out with Covid-19 masks, part of our party attire.

Between songs, Bernie told us she was proud of her portrait hanging on the wall behind us. "It reminds the staff here that I wasn't a dummy. Once I went to college and had a life!"

Despite her wheelchair, she danced wildly!

The staff from the business office across the hall stopped by to see what was going on. Even the administrator's dog poked his head in the door, seeking an explanation and an ear-scratching.

Life is a circle dance, and what goes around comes around.

Bernie grinned when she told us, one more time, about her dance with Emilie, seventy years before.

"June 2022 and we are dancing again!" I said, holding back sobs.

No doubt about it, God did turn our mourning into dancing, just like Psalm 30:11 promised. Bernie was 90 years old. Mary was 61, and I was 79. In an instant, we morphed into teenagers again, connecting as we never did before. Tossing aside vulnerability and holding back tears, we let nothing get in the way of Bernie's Dance.

A Gardener's Perspective

I envisioned a Prickly Pear Cactus when I thought of Bernie. Cacti were rugged, drought-tolerant hombres. Lizards skittering across the desert and javelinas with cast-iron stomachs found them tasty.

Bernie longed for relationships just as a desert flower craved moisture. "I don't have any friends!" she frequently lamented. Her tirades of anger were a coat of needles that kept people from getting close. The behavior that protected her also isolated her. Depending on her mood, Bernie was as delicate as a cactus flower or as sharp as a prickly pear. Her big, brown eyes attracted, but her abrasiveness repelled.

Bernie's roots grew deep in depression and anxiety. "Why do I have so many problems?" she pondered. She turned her face to the sun, a flower leaning toward brighter days ahead.

Chapter Five
Thunderstorms

November 19 was a peaceful day in Colorado Springs in 2021 until my cell phone jangled. The caller ID showed that Prairie View Senior Center in Tracy, Minnesota was calling. I picked up immediately. A facility caregiver where my sister had lived for six years reported, "Bernie's lonely."

This statement didn't knock me over with shock. For most of her life, loneliness had followed Bernie like chronic pain. Declining health, senior living, and difficulty making friends were long-standing companions of my 90-year-old sister. I was relieved to get an update about an ordinary problem, unlike last month's crisis.

Only four weeks ago, Bernie had a mental breakdown that included disorientation of time, space, and reality. Since my sister had fallen in love with an administrator at the facility, she had been upset. The guy, fifty years younger than Bernie, had recently married a young woman on the staff. Bernie had shattered like a dropped water glass.

"I'm dying, and the staff want me to be dead," she lamented on the phone.

Had my sister started some new meds that scrambled her mind?

Another day, Bernie reported, "I've already died, but I've come back!"

No wonder my emotional security alarm went off when I got an unexpected call from Prairie View!

I sighed in relief when Bernie's loneliness was the present concern, not psychosis.

Frenzied, like a captured wild animal, Bernie screamed. "I'm not going to eat in the dining room or play Bingo! I'll show them! I don't need to be in an institution. I can live in my own place like I used to! They just want to make money off me. They won't let me go home because they need business. They locked me up against my will!"

On many days, Bernie was determined not to conform. Occasionally, when she was in an affable mood, she could be gracious and polite. I could never predict her status when I called.

I felt jumpy until I checked her emotional temperature.

It was a December night in 2016 when Bernie fell out of bed and hurt her shoulder. She called 911, and she was taken to the hospital for two weeks. The nurses soon recognized that she could not care for herself. Instead of returning her to the Marshall Senior Center, they relocated Bernie to assisted living. No opening was available except 26 miles from her apartment. The move required my sister leave behind her familiar neighborhood. She was forced to give away her dearest friends, two beloved parakeets. Pets were not allowed at her new residence.

Six years later, Bernie still railed vehemently at the loss of her freedom. Independent living had become overwhelming. No doubt, she needed help paying her bills, getting to medical appointments, and shopping for food.

Bernie insisted every caregiver be fired. "They take my credit card and buy pop for themselves without asking me. They steal from my purse!" This drama replayed like scenes in a bad movie. Supervisors had no way to prove a helper's dishonesty or Bernie's paranoia. When no one wanted to work at Bernie's place, a guardian was assigned to oversee her affairs.

Grateful for the miles separating us, I oversaw the whole nightmare from long-distance.

My big sister declined with each passing month. I suspected she could no longer read the greeting cards I mailed to her. Telling time, following a calendar or using her cell phone were tasks that Bernie hadn't been able to manage in years.

Oh, God, help my sister!

Although I had been sending thinking-of-you cards and calling each week, Bernie did not contact me unless she was enraged. "Why is everyone telling me what to do? I can manage my own life!" she would fume.

Our phone conversations were unnerving. No matter how many times I repeated myself, Bernie couldn't comprehend what I was saying. When I restated my words like a parrot with a one-phrase message, I became exhausted. A decline in hearing and in mental acuity danced together every day, luring Bernie into fog and me into desperation.

A weekly FaceTime session between Bernie and me became a turning point in 2021. An Activity Assistant clarified my words when Bernie didn't understand me. Eagerly, my sister looked forward to our weekly talks. I felt jumpy, fearing she might go into one of her abrasive outbursts and yell at me. Having a supervisor nearby helped me relax. Some Fridays, Bernie's conversation was pleasant, and sometimes it was chaotic.

Bernie's face on my screen moved me…even if she had just awakened, if she mumbled, or if she complained. Sharing childhood memories was how we finally connected.

One FaceTime chat was unforgettable!

I said to Bernie, "I'm writing our family story. I need information about the photos you took at Redfield when you visited Emilie there."

When the activities assistant overheard me mention Redfield, she began to yell.

"Emilie was at Redfield? I was an intern at Redfield in the 60's! I lived on campus, directing physical activities for higher functioning residents."

What began as a routine FaceTime visit with Bernie turned into a horror story that kept me awake for nights to come.

The distraught activities assistant became hysterical, demanding to be heard.

Shut up! I don't want to hear this. Emilie has been dead for thirty years!

I was driven to know the truth. I said nothing to stop the avalanche of rage.

What was Emilie's life really like at Redfield?

I didn't want to block a single, petrifying detail from the Activities Assistant.

I picked up my pen and began to take notes.

Yelling always had made me scared. But writing gave me safety and emotional distance. Reporting catastrophe rather than being the victim of it was less terrifying. That's why I started keeping a journal when I was only 11-years-old.

Our FaceTime assistant rambled on with a story she was compelled to tell.

"There were seven cottages on the Redfield campus. Cottage One was where the highest functioning residents lived. They were slaves, doing the work that staff was paid to do. These adults weren't allowed to participate in square dancing or swimming until their work assignments were complete."

The ranting voice paused and asked hesitantly, "Where did Emilie live?"

"Cottage Five," I replied, cringing at what I might hear next.

With a gasp of relief, our FaceTime assistant pushed on.

"Cottage Five wasn't as bad as the higher numbers. The least functional people lived in Seven. The higher the building number, the greater the disability. That's how Redfield was set up. Residents in Cottage Seven were tied to posts so they wouldn't wander around. They didn't even wear diapers. Interns, on the initial tour of the facility, were allowed to stare at them!"

Our storyteller continued in a voice dripping with indignation.

"I filled out a report about what I saw and gave it to an administrator. Not a single thing ever happened to improve conditions!"

Taking a gulp of breath, the activities assistant poured out details colored with horror.

"Some of the residents were attacked by other residents. Victims of Fetal Alcohol Syndrome were sent to Redfield because there was no other placement available for them in South Dakota. They would blow up in violent outbursts and hurt innocent people."

Oh, God! Was this why Emilie had been taken to the hospital for stitches sometimes?

Our FaceTime assistant's emotions escalated with every detail.

"The admission process at Redfield was haphazard in the 1960's. Screening to determine if a newcomer was appropriate for the school was minimal. Some kids were brought to Redfield because their family didn't want them. During my internship, I met a girl whose mother died. She had been turned over to an aunt who didn't want to raise her. This girl, a normal kid, was admitted to Redfield without testing. By the 1960's, she was a grown woman, and I got to know her personally. She had been at the facility since she was a child. She had adapted well to institutional conditions. Fact is, she didn't know any different lifestyle."

What had begun as an ordinary FaceTime visit with Bernie had turned into a gigantic thunderstorm. My heart was drumming in my chest, and my blood pressure was hammering against my eardrums. I felt both livid and terrified

On my FaceTime screen I studied my sister's demeanor.

How had this outburst from her assistant effected Bernie? Was she as upset as I was?

When our storyteller paused to catch her breath, I seized the moment to check in with my sister.

"Bernie, what are you thinking?"

Heatedly, she retorted, "I'm mad because I'm not getting a chance to talk today!"

Eager to end our conversation, I piped up, "Our FaceTime visit is over for today."

In a voice dripping with cynicism, Bernie lashed out, "Thanks for cutting me short, Sweetheart! You're in charge here. I don't get a say in this!"

Reluctant to end our visit on such a sour note but too shaken to continue, I replied. "Our time is up for today. I have to say goodbye. We'll talk next week."

With trembling hands, I shut down FaceTime, feeling like a dump truck had flattened me.

The weight of the Redfield story had left me gasping for the next breath.

Empowered by rage, I seized my phone and called my daughter.

"Carol, I can't believe what just happened! The activities assistant who helps me talk with Bernie on FaceTime was an intern at Redfield when Emilie was there! She dumped on me all kinds of horrible stuff today!"

My daughter, alarmed at my distress, soothed, "Take some deep breaths, Mom. You'll sort this out. You'll figure out what to do with it. Right now, just try to take it easy."

When I hung up the phone, I was calmer, but I felt no peace whatsoever. I was rattled by scenarios of what Emilie might have experienced. Trapped in the middle of a consuming forest fire, I had no way to escape. Flames moved in from every direction.

How could the Redfield intern of Emilie's era be Bernie's helper today? What right did she have to dump her trauma on

Bernie and me? Was she only thinking of herself, not of the pain she was bringing us.

Confusion, like smoke, suffocated me.

God, what do you want me to do with this? Emilie's been dead for thirty years!

Responding on automatic pilot, I did what I always did when I was overwhelmed. I dug in my garden. Furiously, I uprooted weeds. Savagely, I attacked aspen branches. Sweating my way through brambles, working my muscles to exhaustion, I tilled my soul.

The hollyhocks cheered me on. "You can do this. You will find your way!"

I had uncovered courage. The time had come to turn from digging in the earth to digging into research.

Redfield State Hospital and School had been renamed South Dakota Developmental Center in 1989. An article published in the Aberdeen News on June 7, 2019, announced that "Leaving Redfield", a documentary prepared by Paul Higbee and Ryan Philips, was to be aired on South Dakota Public Broadcasting.

The documentary gave me a glimpse of Emilie's life. A long-term resident spoke about his experience at Redfield before 1970. He said there was no freedom of choice. Everyone had to watch TV at the same time in a group, whether they wanted to or not. Many residents were required to work on the communal farm. Each day was regimented.

Continuing to dig into YouTube research, I discovered a 2021 account of a middle-aged man, a counselor for ten years at Redfield. Overwhelmed, he needed to unload his story.

Breaking down in tears, the counselor revealed he was quitting his job at Redfield. He didn't feel safe there. He had been attacked while working at the facility. Scabs and scratches on his face testified to the brutal assault that led him to the local hospital for several days. He said there had been a decline in Redfield staff, because workers felt unsafe due to violence there.

The counselor did not state the origin of the attacks. He did speak, however of dire work conditions. Fifty jobs were unmanned. Remaining staff were routinely expected to work double shifts. Covid-19 infections caused workers to stay home when they were ill.

Were residents revolting against staff? Were overextended employees taking out their frustration on residents?

With dismay, I remembered the occasional Redfield incident reports I received when Emilie had been taken to the hospital for stitches due to injuries.

Was violence the climate for Emilie when Redfield became her home in 1961?

Further research informed me that after the 1970 Developmental Disabilities Act Redfield began to deinstitutionalize higher functioning residents. Sterilization was performed before patients were sent to less restrictive homes. With this information, my anxiety went wild.

Why did Emilie have a hysterectomy in 1983? Had she been sexually abused? Was she pregnant? Was sterilization required before she was relocated?

Guttural sobs escaped my throat as I remembered my twin sister during the 17 years we lived together at home. Emilie was passive most of the time. Occasionally, she would blow up like a firecracker, pounding her fists on walls and tables in frustration. She never hurt anyone. She did not attack people. Emilie was not aggressive, not the perpetrator of violence.

My family sent Emilie to Redfield expecting that she would receive better care.

Did sending Emilie away hurt her more than help her?

They transferred Emilie in 1989, to a less restrictive environment with less supervision. Her relocation didn't happen until after twenty-eight years of exposure to Redfield.

For weeks, rage and sorrow boiled within me like a steaming tea kettle. Questions, for which I found no answer, assaulted me. Of one thing I was certain. I must keep writing. Digging deeper into family history helped me to grieve. The helplessness I had buried for so long needed to be uncovered. There was more to be disclosed in the narrative that no one wanted to reveal. I determined to trust the story to speak for itself. I decided to tell the secrets that demanded to be heard.

A Gardener's Perspective

Every plant in the garden needed water to survive. A gentle spring rain held the promise of summer blossoms. When a thunderstorm electrified the sky with loud outbursts, I feared destructive flooding. Too much water destroyed innocent seedlings and fruitful harvests.

Serenity was fragile, quickly overwhelmed by catastrophe. People could handle only so much tragedy at one time without going into shock.

Lightening bolted like a bombshell explosion on FaceTime when the staffer had unloaded. Stunned and clinging to the life raft of research, I hoped to survive the storm.

Chapter Six
Redfield Revisited

Road trips with my niece, Mary Maes, were always an adventure. Memorial Day 2022 was no exception. The four-generational family reunion in Rapid City, South Dakota awakened my endorphins with happy vibes. Being labeled "Great-Great Aunty Em" made me feel like a wise elder in the tribe known as the Kopriva Clan.

The holiday behind us, Mary and I drove into Minnesota for a surprise visit with my 90-year-old sister. We had shared an unforgettable day with Bernie at Prairie View Senior Center in Tracy. Not allowing her wheelchair to get in her way, Bernie had danced with us to Patsy Cline. Ballads evoked "the good old days."

Driving back into South Dakota, Mary and I planned our next destination, the Kopriva Angus Ranch near Raymond. The proprietor, Jim Kopriva, was my storytelling nephew who could make me chuckle with his tall tales.

As we were traveling across the prairie, an urgent voice piped up in my head.

Stop at Redfield. It's only an hour's drive out of the way. You've got to see it again.

Redfield, where my twin sister Emilie lived for twenty-eight years was a state hospital and school for the Mentally Retarded. I dreaded going there. I tried talking myself out of the persistent notion broadcasting in my head.

You've got to find out what Emilie's life was really like. Go there now!

My blood pressure surged when I recalled a recent FaceTime conversation with my sister. Bernie's assistant had blurted out memories of her internship at Redfield in the 1960's. The picture Bernie's assistant had painted of that institution had upset me for weeks. I felt compelled to get more information about my twin's experience there. I dreaded what I might find.

This road trip was the perfect chance to do some more research.

My intention was to drive quickly through the Redfield campus, to look from the car window at Cottage Five where I had visited Emilie in 1985. Then we would travel on.

Driving on the grounds of the sprawling facility, Mary and I soon realized we were lost. No street signs or building numbers identified Cottage Five. Befuddled, I stopped the car.

"Can I help you find something?" a curious grounds keeper in an old pickup hollered.

I explained, "We're looking for Cottage Five, where my sister lived thirty years ago. I'm writing our family history, and I would like to see the place again."

The maintenance guy replied from his truck, "Turn around. Go two blocks. You'll find Cottage Five on the left. You might want to go by the Admin Building. They can give you some records for your story."

"Thanks so much for your help!" I replied.

Mary and I headed across campus to Cottage Five, an unimpressive clapboard building that had nothing to say for itself. We drove on to the Admin Building, a stately red brick structure with columns guarding the entrance. Our quick drive through the campus had turned into an intriguing adventure. This was the stuff of fairytales and horror movies.

A helpful employee from the Records Department consulted her computer and reported, "Emilie arrived at Redfield on February 22, 1961. She was discharged to another location on October 31,1989."

The clerk continued, "Emilie's report is over 2,000 pages. I will need your birth certificate as ID before I can give you any info. It may take a few weeks to retrieve the records because our microfiche reader broke down. The new one is on order. I will get the data to you as soon as I can."

Realizing I had stumbled on a goldmine of information, I thanked the clerk profusely. When I said I was writing a family history, she gave me an informative booklet. It was a pictorial overview of the South Dakota Developmental Center, established in 1902.

My research about Redfield now progressed with lightning speed.

In the weeks that followed, I learned that the facility had changed names several times since its inception. Each new name illustrated a broadening understanding of people who didn't fit normal developmental patterns. For example, the original institution was called the Northern Hospital for the Insane. In 1913, the facility became the State School and Home for the Feeble Minded.

The vision of this organization was to segregate folks with learning challenges from the rest of the world. In 1959, views continued to change toward people with disabilities. The facility was renamed to Redfield State Hospital and School. The peak enrollment of 1,199 residents was reached in 1963 when more vocational programs were provided. The 1970's brought the advent of Medicaid. The goal of the program was to teach life skills. To move residents from an institutional environment into normalized community settings was the vision. In 1989, the facility became the South Dakota Developmental Center. That name was still used in 2022 when Mary and I visited.

A couple months passed before I received an email from Redfield informing me that the new microfiche machine had arrived. At last, Emilie's file was available to me. I tried to brace myself for what I might find in my sister's records.

Without a second thought, I began to talk to my deceased sister.

Internal thoughts were a kind of vibe, the way we talked. We didn't need spoken words.

Emilie, help me to tell our story. I don't want to write about you. I want to write with you. I'm nervous about what I will find in your files. You know the truth about what really happened. Help me get to the bottom of the story.

Emilie was silent. She was always silent. After all, she was mute.

I pleaded.

I know you don't have words, Emilie, but somehow guide me.

Many sleepless nights and edgy days passed before I picked up the phone to ask Redfield for the specific data I wanted. Within days, forty-two pages of documents arrived in my mailbox.

"Oh, God, help me!" I implored as I tore open the envelope with shaky fingers.

For years, I pondered what life had been like for Emilie when she left home in 1961. Had she missed her family when she was relegated to a noisy dormitory?

How long had Emilie remembered our voices?

How long did it take for Redfield to feel like home to her?

Familiarity comforted me like a warm blanket as I began to examine the Redfield records. Psychiatric evaluations described the sister I had known so well during our childhood. Notations confirmed that Emilie didn't seem to pay much attention to her environment. She didn't care whether she was with others or alone; she didn't initiate social contact. In 1989, she had been relocated to four different dormitories and didn't seem to notice the change.

Maybe, just maybe, the move from home to Redfield was not as hard on Emilie as it had been on the family she left behind. Was her lack of functioning a curse, but her lack of awareness a blessing?

Amid the files, I found a letter from A. A. Thompson, Superintendent of Redfield, dated February 2, 1961, addressed to the States Attorney of Fall River County in South Dakota, Alan G. Williams. The letter stated, "Emilie was adjudicated as mentally retarded and committed to the State Commission on August 8, 1952. To complete our files for admission, it is necessary that we receive the Findings and Order of Commitment to the Institution and two (2) Warrants of Admission."

Emilie Kopriva had been legally declared mentally retarded when she was only nine years old. That meant my parents had initiated sending Emilie to Redfield eight years before she was finally admitted at age 17.

My parents agonized for years before letting go of Emilie.

A letter dated October 7, 1960, from my mother informed Superintendent, A.A. Thompson that a doctor had examined my sister. Three months previously, he had recommended Emilie enter Redfield as soon as possible. Mom went on to report that Emilie tore her garments. Keeping her properly clothed was impossible. Without further elaboration, Mom urged that Emilie be admitted to Redfield as soon as possible.

There were other health issues in the family. My mother wrote about my father's rapid decline due to Parkinson's Disease. At age 61, Daddy could no longer publish The Edgemont Tribune, and he was qualified to receive Social Security Disability. To top off his reduced functioning, Daddy needed Mom's assistance in feeding and clothing himself. Taking care of both Daddy and Emilie was more than she could handle. Institutionalizing Emilie was no longer an option, but a necessity.

By 1961, Parkinson's Disease had destroyed my father's ability to work and exhausted my mother, his caregiver.

As I read Mom's plea to the Superintendent, I noticed another box of Kleenex on my writing desk had run out of tissues. My tears saturated the Redfield documents. Despite our pastor's advice to care for Emilie at home, the time had come for my parents to institutionalize my twin.

Emilie's admission to Redfield was a painstaking ordeal. Clearly, my parents had not hastily discarded a child they did not want.

Questions lashed me like a corded whip beating my bare back.

Why had my parents taken eight years to complete the admission paperwork?

If Emilie had been hospitalized at age nine, could Bernie have been spared her mental breakdown at age 22?

Working for Daddy each day and placating Mom every night caused Bernie to collapse in 1954. A psychiatric hospital in Denver admitted her initially. During the next ten years, Bernie was in and out of Yankton State Hospital five times. She received psychotropic meds and extensive electric shock treatments.

Bernie could have spent her remaining existence buried alive in Yankton. But destiny had a different plan.

Catching a ride off campus during visiting hours, my sister fled for her life!

She escaped the institution in plain sight in 1964, never to return.

Bernie's FaceTime assistant at Prairie View had said that sometimes relatives dumped unwanted children at Redfield. The institution took kids into the facility without testing them.

My parents had not been in that category. They had struggled for years before sending Emilie away. Deep inside, I felt guilty that I hadn't done more to help the folks.

You should have given up your life so Emilie could have stayed at home!

A rational voice within me argued.

You have your own purpose in this world. You must let go of Emilie and live your life!

Studying a Redfield health summary dated February 6, 1976, allowed me to view Emilie through a professional lens beyond my sisterly perspective.

Clearly, the care facility had offered my twin help that her family could not give.

Upon admittance to Redfield, Emilie was diagnosed with mental retardation and epilepsy. Phenobarbital was given twice a day to control her seizures. Her stumbling gait and her lack of normal knee reflexes were attributed to congenital cerebral spastic paralysis. Further independent study informed me that about 70% of Cerebral Palsy cases resulted from an injury to the brain or a lack of oxygen at birth.

Examining the Redfield files, I found a hodgepodge of details that extended beyond what Mom had told me about our birth. Tears lubricated my fingers as I examined the data.

No good news was to be found anywhere in this tragic summary.

- Mom had been comatose for weeks after giving birth to twins.
- No definite medical cause for Mother's coma cited.
- Emilie couldn't digest cow's milk. (Our grandfather purchased a goat for milk she could process.)
- At age ten, Emilie's left eye was surgically removed. She would not leave the irritating, artificial replacement in place.
- The last epileptic seizure had occurred on May 8, 1989.
- Emilie tore a mattress pad and wet her bed when she had restless nights.
- Emilie could concentrate for long periods, allowing her to sort and string beads.
- Emilie was unable to achieve any of the items on the Stanford Binet Intelligence Test on May 7, 1980.

- The Vineland Adaptive Behavior Scale, administered on August 6, 1985, confirmed Emilie was Profoundly Mentally Retarded.
- Emilie did not initiate interpersonal contact.
- She had no expressive communication skills.

Emilie didn't deserve this! She never hurt anyone! God, where were you?

Goals set by the social development staff included building spoken vocabulary to 13 words, introducing gestures, and increasing group activities.

If I had only thirteen words to use, what would they be?

"Light" and "candy" had been the only words Emilie spoke when we were kids. Gestures told her story when she was mad. Pounding on tables and windowpanes got our attention. Humming at the dinner table expressed how much she enjoyed food.

Early in my review of records, I recognized that Emilie had received more comprehensive care at Redfield than she got at home. An institutional setting had provided the ongoing care her family could not give.

My guilt began to lift when I examined the professional care Redfield had given.

The activities assistant at Prairie View, during her FaceTime rant, revealed that some Redfield residents were sterilized. On hearing that, my imagination had gone wild. I knew my sister had undergone a thyroidectomy in 1982 and a hysterectomy in 1983.

Had Emilie been raped? Was the hysterectomy performed to terminate a pregnancy? Was sterilization required before Emilie could be placed in a group home?

I sighed with relief when I read the surgery reports that I found amid the scattered history. A fibroid uterus and irregular bleeding led to Emilie's hysterectomy.

A 1986 behavioral summary caught my attention next.

"Emilie is typically very passive and compliant. She displays appropriate affect and communicates her wants and needs through facial expressions, gestures, and occasional verbalizations. With encouragement, Emilie will interact with staff and with her peers. For leisure activities, Emilie enjoys watching TV and manipulating cloth. Emilie can concentrate for long periods of time and her attention to detail is impressive. Emilie does not exhibit behavior problems and receives no psychotropic medications. Emilie wears non-tear tops. Still, on occasion, she tears her sheets."

Amid the random documents, I found a visitor sign-in record which spanned the years of Emilie's stay at Redfield. This document caused me to remember Daddy's dying words in 1967. "Visit Emilie just to let the staff know that somebody cares about her. They will take better care of her when they know she matters to us. Drop in unannounced. Then you will see what her life at Redfield is really like."

That Emilie did not know us or could not communicate with us was not the core issue. Daddy's top concern was ensuring Emilie received quality care. He loved her.

Family visits were infrequent and brief. Every minute left an indelible impression on us.

Daddy, the first family visitor, stayed for 25 minutes on July 8, 1961. Mom came a couple times that year, followed by one stop in 1962.

A dear friend from Edgemont, mother of a retarded daughter, had accompanied Mom for a 30-minute visit on August 16, 1964. As regular as clockwork, my parents used to chat with this family. While I babysat Emilie in the evening, my parents escaped. Talking with compassionate friends comforted my parents like nothing else could.

Visitation records revealed I had checked on Emilie on December 30, 1964.

I did not return for twenty years.

When I finished my undergrad studies in 1965, I wanted to get as far away as possible. My cup of sadness was overflowing.

Since I couldn't improve my twin sister's life, I had put all my attention into building my own life. Marriage, family, and career in Los Angeles had filled my calendar.

Emilie's most faithful visitor was Rose. In the summer, she drove her five youngsters to the Twin Cities to participate in tennis tournaments. On the way home, visiting Aunt Emilie was a ritual. Rose didn't want to expose her kids to the grim innards of the facility. So, Emilie was brought out to them on the sweeping lawn.

On Emilie's fortieth birthday, August 5, 1973, Greg and our mother arrived for a visit. A widow since 1967, Mom must have felt especially burdened by memories that day. Nothing had ever been the same for her after giving birth to twins. How different life might have been if both of her babies had been healthy.

The sign-in record showed that on September 2, 1978, Bernie and one of her Minnesota friends visited Emilie.

In 1985, Bernie and I visited Emilie together.

The last family visit took place on May 5, 1989. Our brother, Charles, took Emilie for a walk. She peed her pants shortly after they left the dormitory. Many years later, Charles told me he never went back because Emilie didn't know him. He had felt so hopeless and helpless he never wanted to visit again.

Sadness spilled out my eyes as I reviewed every page of medical and visitation history.

A new chapter began in Emilie's life when she was transferred on October 31, 1989 to a group home, occupied by five developmentally challenged adults. Redfield health professionals were certain Emilie was ready for a less restrictive environment.

Revisiting Redfield and reviewing records sharpened my memory. Emilie became a real person again, not a phantom from my long-ago childhood.

I must continue writing our family story!

My father's words were true, "Emilie matters."

We all mattered. We struggled. We endured. We continued to grow together through the sorrow we had shared. Growth was slow. Emotional healing took years.

A Gardener's Perspective

Like a fine Southern estate, the brick buildings of Redfield Hospital and School sprawled over acres of pristine lawn. Expansive fields created an air of endless possibilities. In contrast, the narrow corridors that housed residents seemed cluttered and confining.

Retardation and mental illness had a cruel way of diminishing horizons and shrinking prospects. And yet, each life mattered. Each flower in the Garden of Eden was cherished, even the weeds and dandelions.

Chapter Seven
Toying with Memories

On an early June morning in 2022, the Relentless Ponderer in my head ambushed me during morning coffee.

What evidence do you have to prove to the world that Emilie really existed? No one talks about her. Are you sure she wasn't a phantom of your imagination?

Stunned by the truth behind this odd query, I caught my breath.

I have nothing at all that belonged to my twin sister...no trophies, no awards, no drawings or letters. I have absolutely nothing that Emilie ever laid her hand on. All I have are a few musty photos in my garage.

Frantically, I began to search from room to room, looking for reminders of my sister. An inventory of the innards of dressers, desks, and filing cabinets, confirmed my initial conclusion.

I have not a single thing that was Emilie's!

Exhausted from looking for memorabilia of my twin sister, I paused to gaze through the window onto my backyard. What a contrast the garden was to the gloom that covered me when I thought about Emilie.

My country garden calmed me whenever I felt blue. Since I moved to Colorado in 2011, it had been my little patch of paradise. Each year, it became lusher and more restful.

When my gaze returned to my bedroom, I was delighted by the Garden of Eden that I have designed inside my home. Pink flowers on my quilt were a pastel fantasy. My headboard, an old garden gate, displayed a straw hat, a seed packet, a kneeler, and gloves, elements of a fairy tale garden.

I rejoiced with child-like wonder at the beauty I had created and chosen to dwell in.

Every nook inside and outside my country cottage reminded me that life was a blooming garden. Lost in reverie, my eyes landed on the picture of the Edgemont house that I had hung on my bedroom wall.

In a flash, I'm five-years-old again, sniffing the yellow roses that line the sidewalk. Counting the 45 trees around our big house on Second Avenue, I see my brother.

"Charles, do you remember our yard and the treehouse you built in the elms? I felt so privileged when you would let me climb up there with you. You were nine when I was only six."

Do you remember, Charles, before life got so scary? Before Emilie's eye was cut out? Before Bernie went nuts?

My reverie eased back to the present. My gaze continued to wander around the bedroom. I was ready to give up searching for a memento of Emilie. Then I noticed just what I'd been searching for, something that Emilie had touched.

The doll crib! Tucked away in the corner, the diminutive bed had become the spot where I stored quilts. Repressed memories had lingered there, too.

Emilie, have you been helping me to write this book?

Have you been inspiring me to see what has been right before my eyes?

To feel what has been locked away in my heart.

Your doll crib is where I've been gathering memories.

Without giving thought to the matter, I had piled manuscripts into the doll crib. It held scattered pages retrieved from the floor, a treasury of Emilie stories.

Another scene rolled across my memory screen.

Emilie held the dolly with the cracked, porcelain face, wrapped in a soft, blanket. Standing near the crib, she had a vacant look on her face. The Mommy-Baby game meant nothing to her.

Disappointed, I took the doll from her and put it in the crib. Walking away, I looked for another game.

Emilie, will you ever play with me? Mom expects us to play together, but you just stand there! If you won't play Baby, let's play School. I love teaching...just like Mom used to do before she married Daddy.

At six, I loved school even though I was in the dummy class because I couldn't read yet. Emilie loved watching from across the room. She understood lots of things, but she couldn't talk about what she saw. She couldn't read either.

I lined up the kiddy folding chairs and the doll rocker in the sunroom, our playroom. The knotty pine walls and the floor-to-ceiling bookshelves made this space feel just like a real classroom. I set up the miniature folding table and put some schoolbooks on it. Porcelain Dolly and Scotty Dog sat in the first row, quietly waiting for the lesson to begin. Emilie stood off to the side, shredding some fabric.

I knew Emilie couldn't sit still very long. I didn't even try to get her to join the other students. Holding a book, I made up a story, pretending to read to my class.

Mom will be happy that I'm keeping an eye on Emilie. That's my job.

Every toy Mom purchased was intended to develop Emilie's hand-eye coordination. As we played together, I was expected to be her occupational therapist. Pastel beads made a cute necklace, and colorful disks formed a chain. Donut rings stacked up to build a tower.

At first, I enjoyed new toys, but after a few months, I became bored with them. Emilie followed my example when I sat with her on the floor. She never started playing on her own. Like me, Emilie wanted to please. Building and balancing toys wasn't of relevance to her.

I'm sorry, Mom. I know you want Emilie to play, so she will stop tearing her clothes. But I can't make her stack blocks or string beads. She just can't do that on her own.

When I wasn't in school, Mom bribed me with treats to play with Emilie. Ice cream, chocolate Ding-Dongs, or Dolly Madison cakes were my reward.

"If you play nice with Emilie, you will have a party this afternoon on the lawn!" Mom's voice enticed.

No matter how many goodies Mom offered me, I couldn't get my sister to play in the little house our grandfather built for us. Instead of playing, Emilie stood apart, still as a pillar. Sometimes she made mewing sounds, like a lost kitten.

What are you thinking, Emilie? Why are you so sad? How can I make you happy? All you do is watch me.

Sunshine, our yellow tomcat, was my buddy. He purred whenever I picked him up and pet him. At least I could make the cat happy.

In 1951, when we are eight years old, Mom purchased a blue doll buggy for Emilie and me for Christmas. I didn't play with dolls much at that age. I had another game in mind for the stroller. Sometimes our kitty allowed me to take him for a ride in the buggy…if I didn't go too fast. When I dressed him in doll clothes, he indignantly bolted away. Being a baby doll was not a tomcat's idea of fun.

Sunshine napped under the Spirea Bush in the summer. He always greeted me with a musical chirp. He was delighted to see me, even though I had awakened him.

Did he know I felt lonely? With a purr, he promised to love me forever.

The Relentless Ponderer interrupted my cat reverie with another question.

What became of the childhood toys that Emilie had in Edgemont?

Dark thoughts sped far beyond the fate of Emilie's belongings. Memories ran like wild stallions, stampeding on the prairie, causing my feelings to tremble.

My mind raced to the last day Emilie was at home. Sadness propelled me to my garage to dig into dusty storage boxes. Eventually, I found a tattered journal that told of Emilie's departure on February 20, 1961.

"There was no public transportation available in Edgemont. The County Sheriff drove up to our house to take Emilie to Redfield, the facility for retarded people. Shame and guilt colored that moment. It looked like my sister was a criminal about to be taken off to prison. But Emilie had not broken any laws.

It isn't Emilie's fault that she is retarded!

Curious neighbors gawked from their windows to watch a police vehicle in front of the Kopriva place.

I felt shame when the sheriff came for my sister. I was relieved when she left.

I don't want to be Emilie's caregiver every day for the rest of my life.

At the same time, I felt sorry for her.

Sobbing my way through the old journal, I heard the Relentless Ponderer again.

"What happened to the toys after Emilie left?"

As soon as this question rolled into my mind, I recalled the answer.

Anything reminding us of Emilie was boxed up and stored in the attic, forgotten for 25 years. In 1987, Rose, purged the Edgemont house of dusty boxes before the property sold. Childhood toys were heaped on the junk pile.

Emilie was hauled away to an institution, and her toys were hauled to the dump!

Relieved of my role as Emilie's caregiver, I became a student at the University of South Dakota in 1961. University life was my first step in breaking away from the family I wanted to forget. Only out of obligation, never out of joy, I revisited my aging parents in Edgemont. I tried to stack barriers between myself and the past. But noises lingered in my memory bank.

Recalling my hometown was like going to an old cemetery full of crumbling tombstones and haunting sounds. My ears remembered the vivid soundtrack.

When Emilie wailed or bawled, Mom announced, "Emilie has crocodile tears!"

Loud farts exploded, and Emilie chortled wildly. Charles had taught my twin to laugh boisterously whenever she passed gas in church. Worshippers would turn to stare when she farted. "That poor Kopriva Family," onlookers mumbled. Mom and I reddened with embarrassment whenever Emilie and Charles played their Game of Farts.

Humming at the dinner table was Emilie's way of saying, "I love to eat!"

Rapping her fist on a windowpane, Emilie told us, "I've had enough!"

Emilie showed emotions noisily, but I stuffed my feelings in silence.

I did not find my emotion voice until much later, when I began to write a memoir.

My calendar proclaimed, "Christmas is just around the corner."

The elves were busy in Santa's workshop. Eight reindeer were eager to pull a sleigh. Toys for Tots commercials blared from the TV. Seasonal hype about toys made me recall the toys I shared with Emilie. I had managed to put aside the baby crib and the doll buggy. But I never put aside the guilt that followed me wherever I went.

A Gardener's Perspective

December 15, 2022

A gentle Colorado snow placed its hand upon my garden like a benediction. The liturgical calendar on the kitchen wall told me Advent had arrived. The time had come to prepare for the birth of Baby Jesus. My thoughts frequently turned to my child-like sister.

Emilie, I knew what you felt, even though you didn't have words to tell me. Help me to put words to my feelings. Allow the ice within me to melt. You've always been my muse.

Gazing out the patio window, I noticed sleepy shrubs, eager for a cup of melting snow.

Week by week, stifled emotions, like dormant seeds, began to unfreeze as I wrote the family story. The weight of responsibility I had felt since childhood began to dissolve.

My winter garden mirrors the thawing within me.

Sun broke through the cloudy sky. Patches of frozen snow began to melt into random puddles. Then my blaring TV predicted another freeze was on the way. Water would soon return to ice.

Melting and refreezing, my feelings were like changing weather. I must forgive myself for being the Well Twin. Feeling guilty was not the same as genuine culpability.

Tears, like melting snowflakes, washed away layers of guilt. I felt sad Emilie had been given no choice. She had been imprisoned by retardation, but I had been freed with awareness. I accepted the new beginning Advent promised me.

Chapter Eight
Little Helpers

How did it happen that I was born in a hearse—a vehicle designed to carry dead bodies, not newborn babies? When I asked my brother, Greg, he searched his memory and came up with an explanation. "The City of Edgemont didn't have sufficient funds to afford both an ambulance and a hearse. With no hospital in our hometown, our local doctor used the only mode of transportation available. He had to get Mom to Our Lady of Lourdes Hospital, twenty-six miles away."

As I probed my mother and siblings for details of my birth story, the drama had become larger-than-life. With each telling, it had become more intriguing and complicated. I had replayed the narrative many times, trying to make sense of it.

The synoptic storyline was vivid.

Emilie and I were born on August 5, 1943. Mom went into a coma for three weeks. The cause of Mom's medical crisis had never been fully explained. My father insisted a specialist from Omaha, Nebraska tap Mom's spine. Mom, near death, had awoken from the coma. Following several weeks of hospital care, Mom was sent home to recover. Mom's 19-year-old sister came from the family farm near Nenzel, Nebraska to manage the household while Mom recuperated.

Unfortunately, Mom never did fully recover from the birthing trauma. One hour after I was born at three in the morning, my sister was born at the hospital. Years later, when I asked my mother to recount our birth story, she told me the doctor had been afraid she would bleed to death. Getting to the hospital before Emilie arrived had been urgent.

Was Emilie's birth delayed to prevent Mom from dying?

My family would never know for sure what happened on that midnight rush to Our Lady of Lourdes. We were, however, certain about the result. Emilie was profoundly mentally retarded and Mom was discombobulated.

"One of the twins is black!" Mom had told a neighbor.

Did Mom think Emilie was the black infant because she was retarded?

Was I the black child because I escaped the birth canal first, causing my sister to struggle?

Preparing meals and keeping house were tall tasks for my distracted mother. I was on my own, without consistent guidance. Fixing my own breakfast meant heating up a cup of milk flavored with Nestle's Quick. Clean school clothes were never a certainty. I couldn't read the clock, so getting to class on time was chancy. Sink or swim, that's how life was for a six-year-old. I didn't know anything different.

Back in the 1940's, there were no mental health or home health care services available in a small South Dakota town. My family tried to get by one day at a time. I thought that's how it was in everyone's house. Surviving was the focus. We put our heads down and plowed forward like oxen pulling a loaded cart.

My older siblings and I had no choice but to grow up fast. Expected to take on adult responsibilities at a young age, we knew what it meant to work hard. Greg, Charles, and Bernie helped in the basement newspaper plant. Upstairs in the family quarters, I scrubbed floors, washed dishes, and watched over Emilie.

Greg told me, in a rare moment of unfiltered vulnerability, a story from his childhood. Masking sad memories with a jovial smile, Greg seldom talked about what life was really like for him as a youngster.

"I was only eight years old when Mom would send me uptown in the afternoon to bring Daddy home from the bar. When the bartender saw me, he would yell out to me across the noisy room, 'Hey, kid, he's not here. He's in the bar across the street.' Daddy would always come with me right away. He would stumble down Main Street as we made our way with townspeople gawking at us."

Despite Greg's usual attempt to paint the past in good-ole-days colors, discord prevailed in the family long before Emilie and I were born.

Family problems preceded us twins. We didn't cause all the pain in our family!

Greg (age eight) dressed in church clothes on his First Communion Day. Mom's favorite child, he provided the emotional support she desired, but did not find in her marriage.

On the international scene, World War II was exploding like a bomb. The conflict in our household mirrored the fighting abroad. Our world was not a safe place to be.

Greg told me that Daddy had brought on three young printers to help with publishing the Tribune. Within two weeks, America entered World War II in December 1941. Daddy's employees were drafted into the army. Greg, at eleven, and Bernie, at nine, had to learn the Linotype keyboard quickly to help Daddy. They went from children to adults overnight.

Bernie operated "the machine" in our basement into her adult years.

We twins were eight years old when hysteria took over.

Washing Emilie's hair became a battle. That's why it didn't happen often. Forced to bend over the bathroom sink, Emilie screamed and jerked away. She thought Mom was trying to drown her. Finally, Mom tore off her clothes and forced her into the bathtub. Emilie, fighting for her life, managed to scramble out of the tub.

Mom, as overwhelmed as my sister, raged at me, "Get over here and help me!" I knew there was nothing magical I could do to stop the yelling. To escape the out-of-control drama, I fled in terror from the bathroom. I ran out of the house, seeking a place to hide. My wildly pounding heart was throbbing in my ears, even louder than Mom's screams.

Abandoning Emilie in the bathroom, Mom charged after me like an enraged bull.

"You just wait 'til I catch you!" she snorted.

I darted across the backyard and cowered behind a dusty sofa in the garage.

That was a mistake. There was only one way out of the garage, the open doorway where Mom fumed. I was trapped.

Within moments, my mother's rigid fingers dug into my arm, causing my body to melt into limpness. I knew I was a goner.

Time and feelings froze.

In horror, I realized that Mom had dragged me across the yard. She had pulled me down the stairs, into Daddy's shop.

"She's not helping me! She ran away when I needed her to give Emilie a shampoo. Whip her for not helping me!" Mom exploded.

In frustration at being interrupted when he was working, Daddy met the moment head on.

He didn't bother to ask me what had happened. He simply jerked off his leather belt.

He beat me!

How long the lashes lasted, I couldn't say.

Scars were imprinted on my back. Both my skin and my spirit were broken that day.

From that time forward, I never felt safe from my parents' unpredictable outrage.

With the birth of twins, my entire family changed forever. Everyone eventually had found a way to cope. Daddy drank. Mom screamed. Charles laughed. Greg worked. Bernie raged. Emilie watched. I disappeared.

I hid from my parents as much as I could, becoming as invisible as possible. In later years, Daddy described me as a timid child.

He was right.

Daddy, did you ever wonder why I had become so quiet?

Despite my best efforts not to cause problems, earthquakes would unexpectedly reach level eight on the emotional Richter Scale of our family. I could never be quite sure when rage would shake the household. But I determined to be safe by staying as far away as possible from my parents.

In 1994, a psychotherapist diagnosed me with Post Traumatic Stress Disorder to explain my jumpiness and anxiety. My childhood war zone taught me to be on high alert. Escalating voices, rapid movements, and violent outbursts had become survival triggers.

My big sister was 11 when Emilie and I were born.

Like the rest of us kids, Bernie became a Little Helper. She was expected to babysit, to clean house, and to help Daddy with the Tribune.

One night, Bernie babysat her little sisters. Our parents had gone uptown to visit the friends who also had a retarded daughter.

It was bedtime. I was three-years old. Sitting fully dressed, in the metal youth bed I shared with Emilie, I was whimpering.

I couldn't get my high topper unlaced. The shoestring had a tight knot that wouldn't budge to my small fingers.

Finally, Bernie came.

Scolding me, she impatiently removed my shoe.

I drifted off to sleep with my daytime clothes still on.

I knew I was naughty, nothing but a big bother.

While I washed dishes, my mother told me about her growing-up years.

With her nine siblings on the Nebraska farm, every kid was a Little Helper.

Mom's job was sewing clothes for the whole tribe.

"I made all the boys' work overalls and dress shirts," she declared proudly.

"The Stasch farm ran smoothly, and the house was tidy. Not like ours."

Mom was ashamed of our family!

Bernie, Charles, and I were a disappointment to Mom.

Greg was her comfort, a dependable, loyal son. He was never included in Mom's tirades.

Brother Charles was a blond, blue-eyed charmer at age four.

A shy six-year-old, I was a caregiver since I was able to walk.

Being Mom's Little Helper meant that I was her captive audience when she needed to vomit resentment. My mother had never forgiven some dark periods of her life. During the early years of marriage, Uncle Marc, Uncle Rich, and Gramp moved in to help with the newspaper. Mom cooked, cleaned, and washed for Daddy's messy brothers in their crowded apartment. Mom felt like a slave, and she told me all about it.

Feeling helpless, I kept my mouth shut about what my mother unloaded. Mom resented Daddy's prioritizing his family of origin, truth be told.

"Don't tell" was the family rule. I was bound to secrecy.

When Greg talked about our family history, he used to say, "Things really got bad when the twins were born!"

If Emilie and I had never been born, would our family have been happy?

A drill sergeant that was Bernie's role when I was little. She couldn't cook or clean to Mom's satisfaction. However, she was my mother's Little Helper when she supervised Charles and me, making us toe the line.

I was seven and Charles was ten.

Bernie posted a task list on the kitchen wall. We had to finish our chores before playing with the neighborhood kids.

Charles and I had another plan. We snuck away from home without completing our chores.

Bernie came looking for us, yelling all the way.

She dragged me home as I squirmed to escape.

Grabbing a one-inch-thick window shade roller, my sister struck me repeatedly.

"Why don't you whip Charles, too?" I sobbed when Bernie finally put the rod down. Nonchalantly, Bernie replied, "Charles, has sinus. He's sick. I can't whip him."

I knew in my heart that was a lie. Truth be told, Bernie was scared Charles would fight back. So, I got whipped, and Charles went scot-free!

Even prior to the incident with the window shade, I often felt uneasy when I was around Bernie and Mom. I never knew when all hell would break loose. It didn't happen often, but when it did, I hid.

"God, get me out of this house!" I prayed.

I don't know how old Charles was when he became a Little Helper. As a toddler, he would sit on a stool near the Lynotype, while Daddy worked. When Charles would get sleepy, Daddy would carry him upstairs to his crib.

By late adolescence, Charles had become the official photographer for the newspaper. With a new Polaroid camera, he would rush to the scene of the latest catastrophe. Subscribers loved black and white shots of highlights around town.

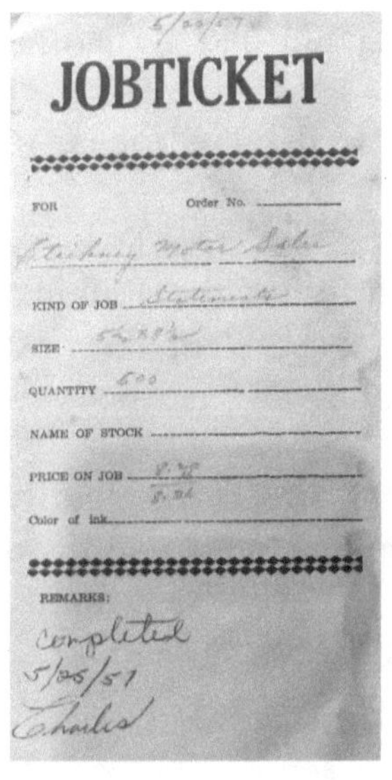

JOBTICKET

FOR Order No.

KIND OF JOB Statements

SIZE

QUANTITY 600

NAME OF STOCK

PRICE ON JOB

Color of ink

REMARKS:

completed
5/25/57
Charles

Skilled at the hand-fed job press, Charles printed flyers and billing statements for local merchants. He was 16, a junior in high school when he completed the job on the left. He knew the newspaper trade inside and out by the time he left for college in 1958.

When Charles went away to college, Emilie and I were 15. We were 17 when Emilie was institutionalized. The only kid left at home, I felt awkward around my parents. I had spent many years hiding from them, trying to be invisible.

Sometimes Daddy would say, "Emmy's a hustler!" I felt like a million dollars when he praised me for being a good helper. I had become a perfectionist and a workaholic just to prove my father was right. At that time, I had found my value in the work I did. Not until years later, would I find self-worth apart from accomplishments.

When Parkinson's Disease got the best of Daddy, Charles postponed medical school to sell the Tribune to another publisher. The era of the Kopriva family newspaper came to a solemn end, and so did Daddy's health.

A Gardener's Perspective

As I looked from my bedroom window, I observed my country garden had a lush carpet of clover spreading over the ground. Plants had chosen their friends. Dandelions, Lamb's Ear, and Yarrow huddled together in the dark earth. The wildness of the landscape, not controlled by Weed Gard, had a natural intention, to cooperate and to thrive.

In the Kopriva household, we had a driving focus, to survive.

Our efforts followed a predictable pattern. On Tuesday night, Mom sat at the dining room table and folded the Tribune. Downstairs in the printshop, I bundled newspapers for the post office and the train station. The Fall Fiver County Newspaper was delivered each Wednesday, right on time.

We were all Helpers, laboring together in the family business. To inform the public of the happenings in a small town on the plains of South Dakota was our job. To grow as a family through seasons of draught and flood was our sacred task.

Chapter Nine
Hungry for Love

October 31, 2024, found me in Edmonds, Washington at Cedar Creek Memory Care visiting my brother Charles. It had been thirteen years since we'd been together. My son, Jim, and daughter-in-law, Gretchen, had flown with me from Denver to the Seattle/Tacoma Airport where we rented a Sienna and travelled forty miles in wet darkness.

Was there any weather in Seattle other than rain?

We arrived at the Best Western on Halloween, just as ghosts begin to wander the streets, accompanying young trick-or-treaters. An adventure was just what I was seeking. Little did I know, chilling memories would soon haunt me like spooks.

Charles was a grease monkey, no doubt about it. He was never happier than when puttering with an engine of some sort. The first contraption, which he had put together when he was ten, had been an old washing machine motor mounted on two-by-fours. Fitted into a bed frame, it had been supported by four wagon wheels.

As a wide-eyed little sister, I observed his race car. Plugging my ears against the banging motor, I watched him chug around our backyard and down the alley.

By the time Charles was a senior in high school, he upgraded to a Model A Ford pickup that he painted red and black.

When he drove to school and about town, girls would chorus excitedly, "Here comes Charlie!"

Pat Keller's auto shop across from the Kopriva house was one of my brother's favorite hangouts. He began to spend more hours pumping gas and patching tires than helping Daddy with the Tribune.

Putting his foot down firmly, Daddy stormed, "Working for me is your real job. Get home and get busy where you're needed!"

A 1929 Model A Ford was propped up for repairs in our backyard.

The print shop was my brother's first exposure to greasy engines. I don't know how old Charles was when he became a Little Helper. My older brother, Greg, recalled when Charles was a little kid he would sit on a stool near "the machine" while Daddy set type.

Charles proudly displayed his space-age rocket, ready for a trip to the moon.

By late adolescence, Charles had become the official photographer and reporter for the Tribune. Using the latest technology, the Polaroid camera, he would rush to the scene of any auto accident or house fire to capture the catastrophe in images as well as in words. Skilled at the hand-fed job press, Charles often printed flyers and statements for local merchants. He knew the newspaper trade inside and out by the time he left for college in 1958.

When Daddy could no longer run the printshop because of Parkinson's Disease, Charles left medical school for a month in 1960 to sell *the* newspaper to a rival publisher who had elbowed his way into our town. Thus ended the era of the Kopriva family business and ushered in Daddy's declining health.

Since Charles and I were only three years apart in age, we were on campus together at Edgemont High School for one year, 1957-1958. My brother was the popular Senior Class President, while I was the timid freshman, who eventually became President of the Latin Club.

I felt like a privileged confidant the day my brother told me, "Myrna is really good-looking…I just love her long hair!"

Shyly, I replied, "Buzzy, the kid who pumps gas at the Conoco is cute. That aqua Volkswagen Bug he owns is something else! I watch him drive home every night after work."

To have a brother, whom I could trust with my secrets, exhilarated me. I couldn't confide in Mom. She was too weighed down cleaning house and overseeing my sister, while I was at school.

Mom was scattered. She had a hard time getting meals ready. From our early childhood, Daddy did his best to see that Charles and I had something to eat.

Our father stocked up on cases of canned soup, Spam, and vegetables, which he stored upstairs in an extra bedroom. Daddy showed Charles how to use a can opener, so we wouldn't go hungry when Mom hadn't prepared a suitable dinner. Managing our household was more of a challenge than she could handle.

We learned to get by despite her limitations. Having clean clothing to wear to school was never a certainty for Charles and me. A couple of ragamuffins, we took care of ourselves as best we could.

No wonder Charles and I both became captivated with food. As small kids, we never knew where our next meal would come from. It wasn't that our family was poor; Daddy was a good provider. Even though our refrigerator was stuffed with eats, items were often shriveled or moldy.

Mom was a good cook when she wanted to be. When company was coming, she delighted in presenting an artful menu. Usually though, she was overwhelmed by routine chores. She simply couldn't prioritize dinner when Emilie was tearing her new shirt or Daddy was inebriated at the Igloo Bar by mid-afternoon.

Fear of starvation came to my awareness gradually. As a student at the University of South Dakota in 1961, I heard my college chums grumble about the food. They described the dining hall menu as "boring, same-old-same-old garbage".

This food is great, and there's even enough for seconds!

In my freshman year, I added five pounds to my petite, 110-pound frame. Being active and healthy, I had high metabolism that compensated for my overeating. Not until mid-life did excess calories appear on my protruding belly.

Beyond college, I developed the habit of carrying food with me in the trunk of my car.

Just in case I became hungry, while I was out-and-about.

"Always Prepared" became my motto. Truth be told, I was afraid of hunger.

To avoid that anticipated rumbling in my gut, I carried Zip Locked veggies, my survival kit.

During a trip in 2000, my daughter had a good laugh when she glanced in my suitcase.

"Hey, Mom, what are you doing bringing ten pounds of Granola to Australia?"

"Just in case I get hungry along the way," I replied nonchalantly.

Doesn't everybody worry about getting hungry?

Charles delighted in cooking a juicy steak for dinner. A thick slab of meat, greasy potatoes, and red wine to slosh it down… that was the best way to end the day. Food, like a narcotic, brought a feeling of well-being.

Unfortunately, the afterglow of a savory meal didn't keep emotional hunger from gnawing. Long-term hunger and short-term gratification became the rhythm, the background music of daily life.

At 45, postgraduate psychology studies helped me understand eating disorders. Through intergenerational family dynamics, I recognized my mother's challenges with food and caring for her family. Viewing my childhood through Mom's glasses, I understood how devastating the experience of scarcity had been for her.

Mom was the middle child of ten kids, raised on a farm. Frugality and careful household management were values she inherited from her mother. When the Great Depression arrived in 1929, every penny had to be counted.

Lack was evident across the nation. Food production declined, and prices soared. My mother never got over the trauma. In her elder years, she refused to pay 89 cents a pound for fresh tomatoes. She recalled the day when the price tag was 19 cents.

No one took food for granted during the thirties and forties.

Struggling through hard times overshadowed Mom's meal planning all the rest of her life. Our dinner consisted of short ribs in a pot of boiling water. Potatoes, an onion, a bay leaf, and some cloves floated in fat.

I used to sneak out to the kitchen, open a can of corn, and gulp directly from the tin.

Anything was better than greasy soup! At least I wouldn't get hungry at school.... not this afternoon.

I was eight years old when Charles learned to fry hamburgers from watching old "Popcorn Charlie" at his snack shack on Second Avenue. When Charles fried a burger, he made one for me, too. Both of us grew up knowing we couldn't count on Mom for nurturing.

Greg would pipe up with his own memories. "It was only following her critical illness that Mom began to struggle with cooking. She used to be tidy and on top of things, when I was little. She was president of the Altar Society at church, and she helped Daddy with the newspaper."

New Year's Eve of 1984, I timidly slid into the back row of my first Overeaters Anonymous meeting. Daddy's drinking had always shaken me, and I didn't know how to make my life secure. Eating sweets when I was angry made me feel better. Stuffing my stomach helped me stuff my feelings.

By my mid-forties I discovered the serenity of OA and the ability to stop hoarding or abstaining from food. Prior to that time, I didn't realize it was possible to eat half a donut rather than devouring four at a time.

If food is before you, grab it! You don't know where your next meal will come from.

The group support of OA, Al-Anon, and Adult Children of Alcoholics gave me courage to change self-destructive scripts from childhood.

My older siblings, Greg, Bernie, and Charles got emotional support from Daddy. They were always rubbing shoulders with him in the print shop. But Mom had no emotional support to give me. Food was my way to fill that void.

"I love you" was too awkward to say in our family. Charles and Daddy used crazy nicknames instead.

"Hey, Sonny, go uptown and buy me some more Prince Albert."

"Okay, Daddus Pup," Charles replied as he headed out the door.

Most of the time, I wasn't on Daddy's radar because I didn't hang out in the print shop.

When Daddy said, "Emmy's a Hustler," I burned with embarrassment. I wasn't used to attention for my hard work.

I assumed that the chaos at the Kopriva house was happening in the families of my classmates, too. I had no sense of normalcy, only my own experience to draw on.

Not all memories were colored in gray. Fun times, when I tagged along with Charles, played on my memory screen. One adventure was like an action film playing in 1950 in Calland's Movie Theater on Main Street.

Back in the day when eight-year-olds ran free, without worry of kidnapping or violence, I tagged along after my 11-year-old brother Charles. Sticking closer than a burr on a dog's fur coat, I followed him past City Park. At the underpass of the Burlington Railroad, we screamed to hear our voices echo off the concrete walls of the dank tunnel.

"Hello! Hello! Is anyone here?" we shouted.

The light at the end of the tunnel guided us into the neighborhood where Mrs. Sweeney's house was located.

We had no intention of finding the housekeeper, who had worked for our family years before. We were drawn to the hamlet of Cottonwood out of boredom on a Sunday afternoon.

Crumpled food wrappers and smelly feces revealed that bums had found shelter within the tunnel. They occasionally hitched a cross-country ride in a box car.

With some trepidation, Charles and I recalled a bedraggled hobo, who knocked at our kitchen door looking for a handout. Mom asked him to wait outside, while she prepared a sandwich for him to take on his way.

Strangers did not come to our door often, just often enough to keep us on our toes at the Burlington Tunnel.

Emerging from the underpass, my brother and I saw the dilapidated suspension bridge swaying in the breeze. To get into Cottonwood, we had to cross the river.

Charles took off running like a racer at full speed. When he reached the middle of the bridge, he stopped to catch his breath.

Then he ran lickety-split to the other side. The walkway swayed like an 8.0 earthquake.

"Stop running! Wait for me!" I shrieked as I clung to the rusty cables. In acid terror, I inched my way. I crawled on my hands and knees on splintery planks. Peering between loose boards, I watched the Cheyenne River, nonchalantly trickling far below.

Charles cackled with delight that I was spooked.

Cottonwood, on the other side of the river, was no more than a cluster of clapboard cottages. Neat rows of fenced vegetable gardens and scattered rusty car parts broke up the quiet landscape.

It was a snapshot of life in rural South Dakota in the 1950's when kids could be kids during summer break from school.

By 2024, the renovated suspension bridge to Cottonwood was stable, with no more splintered wood.

When I visited Charles in Edmonds, Washington, he was 84, and I was 81. Sharing scenes from the "Good Old Days" brought both tears and laughter. For Charles and I, our core curriculum came not from far-away schools, but from within the walls of our family home. Sorrow and joy prepared us to support folks needing the food of kindness.

Horace Greeley, founder of The New York Tribune, encountered frequent stories of hardship in his newspaper reporting. He concluded, "Great grief makes sacred those upon whom its hand is laid. Joy may elevate, ambition glorify, but sorrow can consecrate."

A Gardener's Perspective

Plants required water, sun, and pruning. Without these, a garden struggled to survive. Only when Mother Nature's provision was sufficient could a garden blossom.

Likewise, children thrived when basic needs were met. To bloom, both plants and kids needed adequate nurturing.

Step Nine of Alcoholics Anonymous promised recovery to those who walked the road from addiction.

> "We are going to know a new freedom and a new happiness. We will not regret the past nor wish to shut the door on it. We will comprehend the word serenity, and we will know peace. No matter how far down the scale we have gone, we will see how our experience can benefit others."

Charles and I knew scarcity. Times of lack allowed us to appreciate times of abundance. Together we raced through dark tunnels and across rickety bridges.

We helped each other to trust the seasons. During freezing Winter, we knew that Spring was on the way.

Chapter Ten
Thanks, Daddy

Following a 1986 trip to Edgemont in search of inner peace, I parked my rental car near the Custer Chamber of Commerce on Main St. I'd just visited my father's grave that morning. I couldn't drive another mile without recording my static-like thoughts.

Memories met me on a park bench.

Unabashed words poured into my journal. A letter to my father had been waiting to be written for 20 years, ever since his death in 1967.

Custer, South Dakota
Monday, August 11, 1986

Dear Daddy,

After spending yesterday and this morning in Edgemont, I found it hard to leave there. I came home to remember, to visit your gravesite, and to ponder. I walked the streets of Edgemont and Hot Springs. I felt no release. I searched for you, longed for you, and recalled a million memories.

At Mass this morning, I thought of you when you were ill in the confessional. Sometimes you sat in the sacristy during Mass. You were too shaky to sit in the congregation.

I love you, and I need you to be part of my life today. I never knew you as a friend or confidant like Greg and Charles did. I never heard you say, "I love you." I needed that...I still need it. I can say it to you today, and I do.

I am grateful that you worked so hard for us, planning financially for Mom, Bernie, and Emilie. You taught us to work hard. You called me "The Hustler" because you saw that I worked hard, too.

But you didn't teach us to play or to have fun. Maybe you didn't have enough energy or desire left for that. I felt guilt that you never took time for yourself, never had a hobby or an escape. Visiting Blind Tom and talking things over with Gramp were your way of relaxing.

I feel sorry about your drinking. I don't know the details of when it began, but I know it was a way to escape. I feel guilty about the sorrow in your life: Mom, Bernie, and Emilie.

When I see your grave surrounded with weeds, I wonder what life's purpose is. Is it worthwhile? Alone, forgotten among grasshoppers and rattle snakes, your body rests on a quiet knoll. Brambles and plastic flower overlook the town you built for twenty years.

Why did you die when you were 68? Why couldn't you have lived longer, like the banker, many additional years? Would I have gotten to know you? Would you have been happy?

Daddy, I need you today in 1986. Wherever you are, put your arms around me and hold me close. Stroke my hair and tell me, that you are proud of me.

Know that I love you. I'm sorry I never told you so. You needed to hear it, too, and I never said it. Forgive me for that.

Whenever I write, or give a speech, or talk to a group, or teach a class, I remember you. . .you taught me to appreciate the power of the written and spoken word. I am grateful to you for that.

I withdrew from you and Mom as a child. That was my way of coping with pain. You were always preoccupied with other problems, and I didn't want to be in the way.

When I was in high school and college, I remember your concern that boys treat me right. That was an awkward topic for you to initiate, but you did caution me. I appreciate your paternal care. You wanted to prepare me for the ways of the world.

April 10, 1954, is etched in my memory, a day marinated in joy. You bought me a shiny girl's bike at Coast-to-Coast Store. You didn't think I was safe chasing in the streets at night on foot. Charles played Ditch'um with neighborhood boys, and I tagged along behind. The bike was your idea. I don't recall asking for it.

You looked after me.

You bought me a piano, and I started lessons at 11 years old. I don't recall asking for that blessing either. Making music was a real catharsis when I was frightened by all the chaos in our family.

Thank you for all these things: financial provisions for the family after your death, your hard work, your example of faith through excruciating suffering.

One of my tenderest memories of you is how you knelt by the bed each night to pray. This was a practice you learned from your mother when you were a small boy. You didn't preach religion to us. You had a quiet, steadfast faith in God that shaped my life.

You suggested that we say the family rosary together when times were bad with Bernie. But Mom didn't want to do that, so we didn't.

What a difference family prayer might have made to break down barriers, build unity, and heal hurts.

You were a gentle man. You always spoke softly when you mentioned your mother. You wept when you needed to recommit Bernie to the mental hospital. My heart stood still with sadness when I saw your tears.

When I was five years old, you began to occasionally hide Tootsie Rolls on the printshop table for Charles and me. You were tickled at our delight at finding them.

You loved and respected your father, and you believed in God. "Once you get away from the Sacraments, it's hard to get back," you cautioned.

You were an alcoholic, but you stopped drinking when Greg's wife, Rose, began to encourage you. She made a healthy breakfast, just for you, at her house each morning. Greg would pick you up and take you there. Love was the diet that turned your life around, even more than Rose's bacon and eggs did.

I'm glad you were born on Lincoln's birthday, February 12, 1899. You remind me of Lincoln because of your respect for education, speaking, writing, healthy government, honesty, and courage.

Pray for me. Help me to be free from the past but never to lose respect for it. Wherever you are, I wish you happiness.

Your loving daughter,
Emmy

After I came across my letter to Daddy, I felt inspired to include it in my memoir.

The Internal Pondered wanted to talk with me

"What do you have in your house today that belonged to your daddy?"

"His tobacco can! And, I know right where to find it," I replied proudly.

At once, I retrieved the tin can from the guest closet where I stored memorabilia.

"I have some letters, some editions of The Edgemont Tribune, and photos, too," I tell the Ponderer.

How close-at-hand we keep items belonging to people close-in-heart.

I never really had a "hands-on" experience of my father because my family chores were about helping my mother.

From a distance, I observed Daddy closely throughout my seventeen years at home. I could almost reach out and touch his pain.

Daddy, you were a Christ figure for me. Like Jesus carrying his cross to Calvary, you were a man of sorrows. (Isaiah 53:3).

My father seldom yelled.

I saw him weep and pray on his knees at his bedside at night.

His quiet faith taught me more about spirituality than any catechism ever did.

I was ten years old on a hot July night. Stretched out on the cool grass,

I was about to fall asleep. Daddy's and Gramp's voices droned in the sultry air, like a sleepy bedtime story.

Sitting in a lawn chair in the front yard, Daddy often poured out his heart to his dad, Charles Joseph Kopriva. Gramp was a wise confidant when Daddy needed to talk. My father shouldered many problems, with no relief in sight. Mental illness and retardation did not vanish despite all his best efforts. Troubles lingered forever in our family.

But miracles happened, too

A quiet summer night, Daddy reminisced with his father about a life-changing event. Albert Nelson wore an aura in our story. His profound influence moved Daddy whenever my father spoke of him.

My parents moved to Edgemont in 1939. The dry South Dakota climate soothed the pleurisy that had troubled my father's lungs in Wisconsin.

The local newspaper, The Edgemont Tribune, was up for sale. The current owner, George F. Walters, was dying of cancer, and he needed to unload his business. Daddy worked as an employee for a few months. A printer's salary was meager, and times were tough in the Great Depression years. No way did Daddy have collateral to buy The Tribune.

The scuttlebutt around town was that a wealthy rancher lived in Red Canyon, a short drive from Edgemont. Locals respected Mr. Nelson, a hard worker and a man of integrity.

My father approached him for a loan of $20,000, a small fortune in that era. The deal was settled, not with a legal document, but with a handshake.

Money was tight. My father defaulted on the first installment, despite his hard work. Payment was a few weeks late.

"Pay me back when you can, Lawrence. I don't want your newspaper," Albert Nelson stated matter-of-factly.

The Tribune flourished under Daddy's diligence. Advertisers and subscriptions increased in record time. Soon my family built a large house and newspaper plant at 212 Second Ave.

Mr. Nelson saw in my father what we all saw in him, an honest, humble man. My family recognized in the local rancher a generous man, who believed in the goodness of others. Hope and hard work were the stuff on which my hometown, on the dusty prairie of South Dakota, was built.

Lawrence Kopriva, at his Tribune desk around 1941 (left). By 1961, he struggled to clothe himself because of the trembling and rigidity of Parkinson Disease. (right)

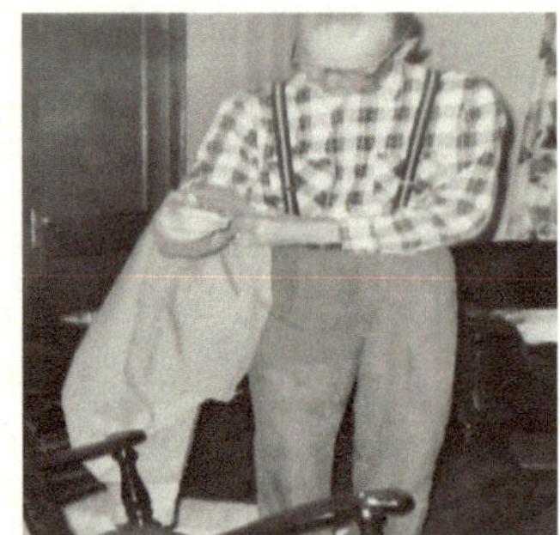

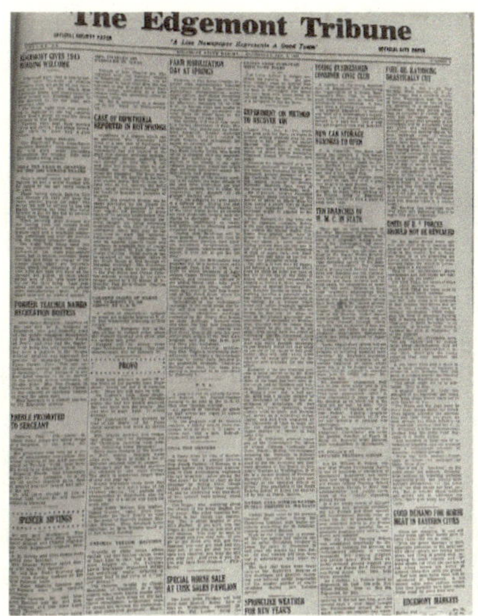
The Edgemont Tribune

The front page of the first edition of 1943, the year Emilie and I were born.

For over twenty years, Lawrence Kopriva was editor and publisher of the Edgemont Tribune.

On January 3, 1949 (when I was five years old), Daddy wrote a business letter to a local county judge in which he described his goal and his code of ethics: ". . .a country publisher's life is not a 'bed of roses,' and like a good judge, he must strive to do what is right and to fight for what is right, as God gives him the light to see it. His greatest compensation being self-satisfaction."

When I was in high school, Daddy paid me to prepare the single wraps. Every Saturday, I printed by hand the address labels from a galley of type. I rolled the 8 x 10 wrapper around each newspaper to be mailed to our long-distance subscribers. Folks who had moved away wanted to stay in touch with the doings in Edgemont.

His purpose in assigning me this menial task was twofold. First, this was a simple job that needed to be accomplished. Second, I needed to learn to manage money. I opened an account at the local bank and began to save my salary of two dollars for college expenses.

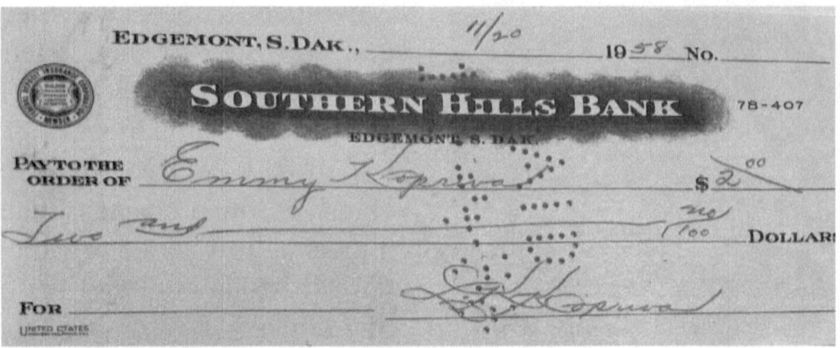

By the time I was 15, Daddy's beautiful penmanship was beginning to suffer. His right hand and overall health were shaky.

Daddy was the first in our family to claim space in the plot on Cemetery Hill.

A portion of the obituary Charles wrote told the story.

In August of 1939, he moved his family to Edgemont and became editor of the Edgemont Tribune. From the start, he professed faith in the struggling little community of 700, and he assumed debts to build one of the largest homes in the town. When his neighbors were somewhat skeptical of his faith in the community, he declared that the future looked bright here and that he intended to stay here and 'live, work, and die here'. He will be remembered by his family as a devoted husband and father, and by his friends as a humble, hardworking, forthright man.

To those words our family proudly resounded, "Amen, so it was!"

My Jesus have mercy on the Soul of

Lawrence K. Kopriva

Feb. 12, 1899 Oct. 20, 1967

O gentlest heart of Jesus, ever present in the Blessed Sacrament, ever consumed with burning love for the poor captive souls, have mercy on the soul of Thy departed servant. Be not severe in Thy judgment but let some drops of Thy Precious Blood fall upon the devouring flames, and do Thou O Merciful Saviour, send Thy Angels to conduct Thy departed servant to a place of refreshment, light and peace. Amen.

May the souls of all the faithful departed, through the mercy of God, rest in peace. Amen.

Merciful Jesus grant eternal rest.

VANDE BOSSCHE'S
Edgemont, South Dakota

SERVICES

10:00 a.m., Mon., Oct. 23, 1967

Church of Saint James
Edgemont, South Dakota

OFFICIATING CLERGYMAN

Rt. Rev. Msgr. J. Weithman

ROSARY SERVICE

7:30 p.m., Sun.,. Oct. 22, 1967

Vande Bossche Chapel

CASKET BEARERS

Jim Bell Bill Schoonmaker
Roy Hudson Wilbur Wing
Babe Highley Tom Bayer

INTERMENT

Edgemont Cemetery
Edgemont, South Dakota

A Gardener's Perspective

Clover thrived in my Colorado garden, forming a green carpet dotted with yellow flowers. It was determined to smother every other plant that got in its way.

Throughout my childhood, I saw my father smothered by grief. Only by steadfastly putting one foot ahead of another did he keep editions of the Tribune in mailboxes.

From Daddy's example, I learned persistence despite adversity.

"Pull yourself up by your bootstraps, forge ahead!" my father directed.

In tough times, I have picked up my shovel and dug in the earth. To uncover hope in the clay of despair required commitment. When storms have overwhelmed me with anxiety, I have turned once again, in trust, to my garden and to my God.

Chapter Eleven
Who's the Guardian?

"Greg, when I'm gone, take care of Bernie and Emilie!" Daddy gasped from his deathbed in October 1967.

"I will, Dad. I will take good care of my sisters," Greg replied.

Daddy's urgent request placed a heavy yoke on the shoulders of a thirty-seven-year-old man who had five children of his own. Because both of our sisters were mentally challenged, being responsible for them was no small task.

For many years, my brothers and I had a clear understanding about our need to look out for Emilie and Bernie. Greg, being the oldest, was in charge. Charles was next in line. I, the little sister, would take over when no one else could. Greg became the primary family spokesperson to oversee Emilie's care at Redfield State School for the Mentally Retarded.

At the time our father passed away, Greg had a dental practice, and Charles was still in medical school. As for me, I was a newly married French teacher at Loveland Junior High in Colorado. Our lives were just beginning as Daddy's life was fading away.

Emilie's life, on the other hand, would never move on. Retardation was a prison from which she could never escape.

On the chilly night when Daddy died, the family tearfully clustered around his bed. Mom, at 62 and in declining health, did not have the stamina to take charge of Emilie's guardianship or other family business. Since my two brothers had a medical background, they were more knowledgeable about healthcare than

I was. I felt secure with them in charge. I was relieved that I was not the one immediately responsible.

While my siblings and I were maturing into adulthood, society was changing its view about the rights of mentally challenged people. Terms like "crazy "or "feebleminded" were not used in medical documents. By 1990, the Individuals with Disabilities Education Act (IDEA) was passed, expanding on the Education for All Handicapped Children Act (PL94-142) of 1975. Individuals could no longer be locked up in institutions just to get them away from the general populace. Those challenged by disabilities were entitled to cost-free, appropriate education in the least restrictive environment possible. They were to be mainstreamed into traditional homes and classrooms suitable for their level of functioning.

Institutions began to revise policies and practices. Across the nation, residents were being moved to domestic settings. To eliminate passing on "bad genes" to the next generation, sterilization was not uncommon. Hysterectomy was not only a means of fertility control, it eliminated menstrual messiness and reduced emotional outbursts due to Pre-Menstrual Syndrome.

Emilie's health was re-evaluated on a yearly basis to assess her capabilities. In 1961, she had qualified for the state benefit of institutional living. Soon after the passage of new legislation, Redfield began to question our family about taking Emilie home again.

What was the most appropriate environment for her social and functional level?

Who was financially responsible for her care, the state or the family?

Did she still qualify for benefits provided by the state?

Would Emilie be safe in a home with only two supervisors?

When I imagined the scene called, "Bringing Emilie into my Family," an emotional power outage enveloped me in darkness.

Could I give up working and move to a larger house for my sister?

Would my marriage endure taking Emilie into our home?

What about finances? My kids would soon to be facing college.

Would Emilie return to a vegetative state, if she were removed from a training program?

My brothers and I had our own families and jobs. We knew very well what caring for Emilie at home required.

Bernie's depression and six episodes of mental breakdown testified to the family strain of caregiving. Bernie had barely clawed her way through life after running away from Yankton Hospital in 1964.

Would I have a mental breakdown if I took over Emilie's care again?

Taking Emilie back into the family was not a realistic solution. Nor was sending her to a group home with less supervision. Greg, Charles, and I were of one mind. Emilie must stay at Redfield.

Rose, too, was alarmed by the Redfield proposal to relocate Emilie. Her worry was coming from first-hand knowledge of Emilie's helplessness. A psychiatric evaluation at Redfield on May 7, 1980, confirmed the family's suspicions. Emilie lacked safety skills as well as expressive communication. In other words, if someone hurt our sister, she had no way to defend herself and no way to tell details to anyone.

Supervision in a group home would not be adequate. From our family perspective, the least restrictive environment was an idealistic vision, not a safe placement for our vulnerable sister.

There was just no easy answer about what to do with Emilie. We turned to our faith to help us. In the Bible, Genesis 4:9, was the Brother's Keeper Principal that required family to care for their own kin. Cain questioned the guardianship issue when he sarcastically confronted God, "Am I my brother's keeper?"

Not to care for our sister at home felt like we were neglecting our responsibility.

But all of us recalled, quite well, what caregiving cost. Emilie needed assistance with basic personal care, such as cleaning herself after using the bathroom. Ugh!

Only those who have cared for a severely disabled person twenty-four hours a day, month after month, year after year, really understood.

Exhaustion and despair had developed a stranglehold within our family. Mom's mental fragility, Bernie's mental illness, and Daddy's Parkinson's were chains which had grown tight. Keeping Emilie at home or sending her away was a decision that had crushed our hearts.

No wonder my parents had spent 17 years sweating blood over this scathing choice!

Suddenly, it was 1961 again. The county sheriff was driving away with Emilie to take her to Redfield. We felt like criminals when we put Emilie in the care of South Dakota.

Now, twenty years later, we felt like criminals all over again when we didn't take her back home.

Am I disowning Emilie all over again? That's what it feels like!

South Dakota wanted proof from me that I was not available to care for Emilie at home.

I provided legal documents and annual accounts to verify that, since 1981, I had been the conservator of my father's brother. Richard Kopriva was in his eighties and in failing health.

Emilie's safety was a troubling consideration that wouldn't go away.

Over the 28 years Emilie had lived at Redfield, I had received notifications whenever my sister was injured and taken to the local hospital for stitches. An incident report was sent to me. This notice was like what parents received when a normal child got a skinned knee at school.

Whenever those letters arrived, I felt like a knife had gouged my heart.

Was Emilie the victim of violence at Redfield?

In all the seventeen years Emilie lived at home, she never was aggressive. She never attacked anyone. She lived in her own small world, not initiating contact with others. She was an observer of life, not a participant, let alone a fighter. In my wildest imagination, I could not picture Emilie starting a brawl.

A sweet-sixteen picture, from around 1960 showed Emilie (right) and me at home in Edgemont. A gentle soul, my twin sister was never violent with others.

Although institutional living was not ideal, most of the time it was satisfactory. Those occasional incident reports from Redfield haunted me.

Was Emilie getting adequate supervision at Redfield?

As I tried to sort out my responsibility to Emilie, the Twelve-Step Program of Adult Children of Alcoholics helped me to find answers. Although I had never been an alcoholic, the roots of our family tree were saturated with alcohol.

When I weighed caring for my twin sister once again in 1981, one slogan from A.A. gave me courage. "You're damned if you don't, and you're damned if you do, so do the thing that's best for you." I felt damned no matter what decision I made, leaving Emilie in Redfield's care or trying to care for her myself. No matter what I decided, there was a gut-wrenching cost.

I couldn't neglect my responsibility either to Emilie or to myself.

Within the Redfield medical records, I located an informative evaluation dated June 9, 1988. The Administrations Placement Registrar had assessed Emilie as capable of living in a home setting rather than in an institution. In reading this report, I saw my sister from the clinical viewpoint of the professional staff. The factual details, listed numerically, made Emilie seem like a case study rather than a real person, my twin sister.

Tears running down my face, I studied the medical report that objectified my forty-four-year-old sister and summarized her limited abilities in thirteen statements or phrases. This was a vivid snapshot of my sister's life.

1. *Medication regulated epileptic seizures, osteoporosis, and thyroid levels.*
2. *Staying on task for thirty minutes, Emilie stuffed envelopes and sorted colors, despite visual limitation.*
3. *Compliant and orderly, Emilie was willing to do whatever activity was presented to her.*
4. *Emilie did not express her needs with words. She hit a window or tabletop with her fist when she was frustrated. No medication for behavior modification had been prescribed.*
5. *Using non-tear shirts and bed sheets deterred Emilie from ripping fabric.*
6. *Emilie could wash her hands, and she was learning to wash her arms.*
7. *Emilie had transitioned easily to four dorm changes within the past two years.*
8. *Emilie rode an exercise bike for about fifteen minutes each night.*
9. *Having limited chewing ability, Emilie ate chopped foods, feeding herself.*
10. *Spinal Kyphosis and Scoliosis did not hinder Emilie from walking.*

11. *Using the toilet every hour prevented Emilie from wetting her clothes. She stuffed the toilet paper roll into the toilet if she was not monitored.*
12. *Sitting in front of the T.V. and paging through magazines was her primary pastime.*
13. *At Special Olympics in 1988, Emilie won a third-place medal at ball throwing.*

Reviewing the report about Emilie's functioning, I learned a couple details I had not been aware of previously.

Emilie couldn't chew well because her jaws didn't function normally. I recalled that when we were kids growing up at home, my sister would grab and gulp her food if Mom didn't fill her plate quickly. I never thought much about this behavior because it was typical for her.

Personal cleanliness, like hand washing and bathroom protocol was hit-and-miss at home. There were so many other family concerns to focus on. Finally, at age forty-four, my sister was learning to wash her arms as well as her hands. She participated in her grooming now.

Tears dribbled down my chin as I pondered Emilie's limited functioning.

Emilie, my heart bleeds for you when I see you through detached, professional eyes.

The question about Emilie's care was finally settled by default. No one in the Kopriva family was available to take over financial or residential responsibility.

Ultimately, Redfield continued to provide care for Emilie as it had done for over twenty years. South Dakota continued to foot the bill. The staff continued to notify us by letter when our sister was hospitalized for an illness, an injury, or a surgery.

The yoke of sadness continued to wear blisters on Greg, Charles, and me. We seldom talked about it because we felt helpless.

A raucous refrain sometimes chastised me.

How dare you have a life? Care you not for your sister?

On most days, a reassuring voice prevailed.

Live your life. Let go of what you did not cause and cannot change. Be at peace!

*A*mbivalent emotions surrounding Emilie's care continued to hum in the background of my mind. Gradually the sound faded.

Not until October 1989 did Redfield find a residence with an opening suitable for Emilie. Greg received a letter informing us that she had been moved to a group home. She resided with five other mentally challenged adults. South Dakota would continue to be responsible for the cost and the care of our sister.

At age 48, at the training center Emilie was assigned the job of stringing beads in the workshop. I was amazed to learn that my sister was able to stay on task for thirty minutes without prompting.

When her left eye had been removed, Emilie's vision had been severely compromised. Records showed that staff had been instructed to approach Emilie on the right side so she could see them coming without being startled. Nystagmus in her right eye meant she had involuntary eye movement known as *dancing eye*. I recalled early days at home. Emilie's eyes wandered all the time, like hungry hummingbirds flitting around a flower bed and never being still.

At age 48, Emilie was working at the training center with a supervisor when Bernie snapped these photos.

At last, Emilie resided in a less restrictive environment than an institution. We hoped that she would be safe and happy in her new home, and we prayed that God would give all of us peace.

A Gardener's Perspective

A Bird of Paradise, large as a tree, loomed at the corner of my California house. I trimmed the broad leaves that wanted to take over the flower bed. Striking orange blossoms, like giant bird beaks, mingled with purple seeds. This rugged perennial commanded full attention of anyone entering my garden.

Greg, the first-born son in the Kopriva family, was an outstanding Bird of Paradise. He was tough enough to shoulder responsibilities. His resolute faith sustained him in caring for aging parents and fragile siblings.

From my early years, I saw Greg as a father more than a brother. I felt relieved that he oversaw family problems. Later, I resisted my brother. He tried to prune my life when I was ready to blossom on my own.

A Bird of Paradise sought sunshine as Greg did when he gravitated toward the spotlight. He loved attention. His professional skill, spiritual leadership, and family loyalty caused him to stand proud as guardian of the Kopriva landscape.

Chapter Twelve
Remembering Mom

We had just buried Emilie on December 9, 1992, at the Kopriva plot in Edgemont when my eyes wandered to my mother's grave. She had been resting on Cemetery Hill for seven months before Emilie joined her there.

When Greg, Charles, and I drove away from the cemetery on that chilly day, my thoughts lingered behind with Mom. Her story begged to be told. I knew I must pick up my journal again.

At age thirty-nine, Mom was no longer a spring chicken when the twins were born. The big house on Second Ave. had been her home, long after her husband died in 1967.

Only when she forgot to turn off the kitchen stove, leaving saucepans to burn dry, did Greg and Rose move our mother into the Rapid City Care Center. Nearly every summer, I traveled from my home in California to see her. Our time together always felt stilted, even though I prayed that we might make a loving connection. But that never came to be. My visits were driven only by daughterly obligation and a heavy heart.

This is the summer to visit Mom. Buck up! Just do it!

One day, I got the notion that interviewing my mother would break through my emotional stiffness in her presence. Mom had always enjoyed talking about the *good old days* of her youth. Recording her story in my journal might be a comfortable way for both of us to pass time together.

Those interviews gleaned a harvest of insights into who Emma Stash Kopriva really was.

Going back to those early journal writings, I realized that her beginnings were typical of a Nebraska farm girl. Born in 1904 on the homestead of her parents, Frank and Emma Stasch, Mom was a middle child in a family of seven girls and three boys.

Mom beamed when she recounted how smoothly the farm ran, like a well-oiled motor. Everyone had a job to do, and they did it to a tee. While the brothers sweat in the fields raising Herefords and sweet corn, Mom kept the Singer humming, sewing Sunday-best shirts for the boys and dresses for the girls.

At the onset of the eighth grade, Emma entered a boarding school, Saint Mary's Academy, in O'Neill, where she resided during the academic year, returning home during the summers to help on the farm. Graduation from Saint Mary's in 1920 had prepared her for teaching in one-room country schools on the Nebraska prairie. She taught for two years in Woodlake, two years in Merriman, and one year near Cody, where she met her future husband, my father.

Nebraska Third Grade Elementary School Certificate

This Certifies

That Emma M Stasch

is authorized to teach in kindergarten to eighth grade inclusive in any school organized under Article 3, Compiled Statutes of Nebraska for 1922. This certificate is issued upon Plan *, is valid for three years and is renewable upon earning twelve (12) semester hours of college credit including three hours in education.

PLAN I—Twelve (12) semester hours of college work including six hours in education earned in a standard college, university or state normal school in this or another state and a minimum grade of seventy per cent (70%), average eighty per cent (80%) earned upon state examination in: agriculture and geography of Nebraska, bookkeeping, civil government, drawing, theory and art, arithmetic, English composition, general geography, grammar, history, mental arithmetic, Nebraska elementary courses of study, orthography, penmanship, physiology and hygiene, reading and public school music.

PLAN II—Graduation from the normal training course of an approved Nebraska normal training high school and examinations as in Plan I.

Given at the office of the State Superintendent of Public Instruction at Lincoln, Nebraska, this 3rd day of August 1926 and valid until the 3rd day of August 1929.

* First issuance First Grade County certificate

№ 1833

John M. Matzen
State Superintendent

Emma's teaching certificate allowed her to earn eighty dollars a month. She smiled proudly, telling me that she always dressed neatly and made sure her hair looked smart.

My Mom became nostalgic when she spoke about the day she had popped into The Cody Booster office. The handsome twenty-nine-year-old publisher, Lawrence Kopriva, caught her attention. A romance blossomed like a rose bush in June. Mom reminisced that Lawrence was proud of the business stationery he designed and the promotional logo he created. "Let us boost your business…it's our business."

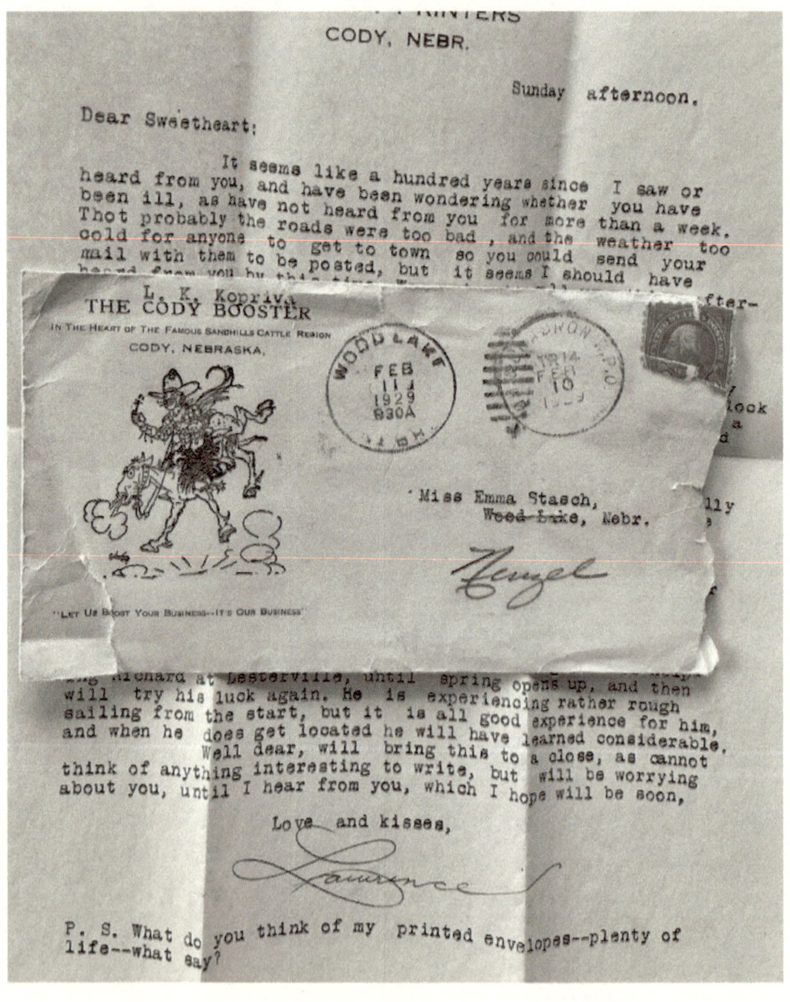

CODY, NEBR.

Sunday afternoon.

Dear Sweetheart:

It seems like a hundred years since I saw or heard from you, and have been wondering whether you have been ill, as have not heard from you for more than a week. Thot probably the roads were too bad , and the weather too cold for anyone to get to town so you could send your mail with them to be posted, but it seems I should have

L. K. Kopriva
THE CODY BOOSTER
IN THE HEART OF THE FAMOUS SANDHILLS CATTLE REGION
CODY, NEBRASKA.

WOOD LAKE FEB 14 1929 930A

FEB 16

Miss Emma Stasch,
~~Wood Lake~~, Nebr.

Hengel

"LET US BOOST YOUR BUSINESS--IT'S OUR BUSINESS"

Richard at Lesterville, until spring opens up, and then will try his luck again. He is experiencing rather rough sailing from the start, but it is all good experience for him, and when he does get located he will have learned considerable.

Well dear, will bring this to a close, as cannot think of anything interesting to write, but will be worrying about you, until I hear from you, which I hope will be soon,

Love and kisses,

Lawrence

P. S. What do you think of my printed envelopes--plenty of life--what say?

With a waning smile, Mom relayed, "In no time, I began to receive affectionate letters, punched out on an old Underwood typewriter on the Booster office stationery."

The courtship of Emma and Lawrence lasted about one year. Saturday night brought them to either the Nenzel Dance Hall or the Cody Pavilion. The Flea Hop and the Charleston were in vogue. Mom recounted, with a tone of regret, that Lawrence had two left feet, and he preferred the slower tempo of the waltz.

Emma Stasch married Lawrence Kopriva at Saint Mary's Church in Nenzel on October 29, 1929.

The New York Stock Exchange crashed on their wedding day! Black Tuesday was followed by the Great Depression, which sank folks into a swamp of poverty for years to come. Next, the outbreak of World War II turned the country and the world into an unforgettable nightmare.

As my mother continued to tell me the family story, I realized what a turbulent era my parents had survived.

Daddy struggled to eke out a living. Finding printers to work on the Tribune was getting to be impossible. Young men were quickly drafted from employment to military service. Daddy's father and two brothers crowded into the newlywed's apartment soon after their wedding. All hands were needed to keep the family business afloat.

"They stayed for three years. I felt like a servant rather than a bride!" Mom had lamented heatedly.

Gregory James was born at the hospital in Valentine, Nebraska on October 25, 1930. My parents' marriage was one-year fresh. Seventeen months later, my sister, Angela Bernadette, joined the family.

After three years in Cody, Mom and Daddy relocated a couple times. First, they settled in Waukesha, Wisconsin. Next, Edgemont, South Dakota became their home in 1939.

Charles Joseph, was born in 1940, followed in 1943 by two unexpected babies, Emilie and Emma.

I could hear Mom's heavy sighs.

That's all she needed, twins to overwhelm an already complicated life!

The thirty-nine years of my parents' marriage had been tightly bound by knotted cords.

My mother's reflections evoked my memories, too.

Back in October 1967, Greg, Charles, Mom and I were wandering through the Edgemont Cemetery. We were looking for the best spot to bury Daddy. Mom was hanging back from the rest of us. She seemed lost in a fog of grief.

At 24, I was a bride of only two months. Maybe that's why I remembered Mom's desolation. The exuberance of my shiny marriage was a stunning contrast to her new widowhood.

I hope my marriage will be better than yours, Mom.

Fifty-six years had passed since Daddy's funeral.

Time had been a harsh master.

The wedded bliss of my youth had been an illusion, ending in divorce in 2002.

A letter I had written to my mother ten years after her death in 1992 had summarized our relationship in a few pages.

Don't Tell!

Tears dripped from my chin onto my writing desk as I reviewed that letter…

Mom, ten years have passed since I wrote to you…and I still want to connect.

I've thought about you several time today, your birthday. If you had lived, you would have been ninety-eight-years old. Next month will be the tenth anniversary of your death.

I have always felt sad that I never knew you. I always wanted to connect with you, but I couldn't make it happen. I was scared to push too hard for a relationship with you. I feared if I couldn't reach you, I would feel even worse. Perhaps you gave me all that you could. You didn't seem to have much to give.

I never heard you say, "Emmy, I love you." I longed to hear those words from you. I blamed myself that you couldn't say them. I'll never forget the one time I told you those words.

I was in college. I had dutifully called home for a Sunday-night check-in. We had run out of platitudes. I knew it was now or never.

My heart was racing, and my palms were damp when I said, "Mom, I love you." You paused. In the silence, I waited for your response. After what seemed a week, you responded, in surprise, "Oh, thank you, Emmy!"

I hung up the phone in dismay. My emotional fuel tank registered Empty. I never said those words to you again.

When I was a little girl, you never held me, Mom. You never read to me. You never hugged me. How I craved your attention. "Please notice me," I begged silently.

Although you didn't touch me, you did use your words to admonish me. I did get attention from you when you were upset. You told me, "If you continue to frown, your face will grow that way." And you were right—my face did grow that way. I have two frown lines above my nose, just as you predicted. Did your prediction cause them, or would those creases have been there anyway? I don't know.

Your admonitions were frequent, but I didn't always pay attention to them. You used to tell me sternly, "Don't kiss the cat. Cats are dirty. You will get germs!" But kiss the cat I did, repeatedly. I loved cats. They were my best friends when I was growing up. And it's natural to kiss those we love.

Why could you never kiss me?

Do you remember how Charles and I used to sneak the cats into the house when you were uptown? A couple times you caught us. Raging through the house, broom in hand, you chased those terrified kittens. Through the living room, dining room, and kitchen they fled. Finally, they escaped through the back porch.

When I balanced the emotional books of our relationship, Mom, I came up with debit. So much was lacking. But, in fairness, there were assets, too. From you I learned the "fear of the Lord." Your God was a condemning judge. Thankfully, my God is less hostile than yours. We both knew that God was our priority. You were the first person to imprint that message on me. I was grateful for that priceless lesson.

When I grew up, I married and moved far away from home. I visited you once a year, because I was a dutiful daughter. Each time I came to see you, I prayed that somehow, this time, we would connect. But we never did. I dreaded our good-byes. Each time I left you, I feared you would die before I would return. I wanted to depart as quickly as possible. Feeling both sad and relieved, I hastened away from you.

One farewell stood out among the blur of all the rest. You were in the nursing home, sitting on the bed. As I was about to leave your room, you said to me, "Take your Guardian Angel with you, Emmy!" That was like a benediction to me. It meant that you cared, and I needed desperately to know that you did. The one thing you had to bequeath to me was your faith. Perhaps that's the most important gift you could give me, if not love. Perhaps that's the only way you could express love.

I am nearly 59 years old now. When you were my age, I was 21. You always seemed old to me. We seldom shared any girlish moments. I always thought of you as dying, not living. You were 38 when I was born. I dreaded the thought of your dying. I didn't want you to leave me. That would mean we would never, ever connect. That would mean our chance would be gone. But was it?

On May 30, 1992, you died.

I was shocked when it happened. I was in Colorado Springs for my son Jimmy's graduation from the Air Force Academy. My heart was spilling over in pride for him and all he had accomplished. Greg called on May 28 to say you were in the hospital. "Are you coming home?" he asked over the phone. My answer was clear, "No." I thought to myself, "Oh, come on Mom, in the hospital again?" I was annoyed that you were sick just when my family was enjoying a celebration. Of course, I wouldn't come home. You would be out of the hospital in a few days. I was certain. That's the way you did it in the past. You were sick, and then you were better. I asked myself, "Why should I go home? We never connect anyway. I just feel awkward." So, I didn't fly home this time.

You surprised me, Mom. You died. I've never allowed myself to feel guilty about my decision not to come to you. Greg was there, your steadfast support.

As I looked back on your life, I always felt like you were trapped in unrelenting circumstances. You were in an unhappy marriage. Leaving was not an option for you. Your religious training admonished that marriage was forever. And then, there was Emilie, your retarded daughter and my twin sister. She would never develop mentally beyond the level of a two-year-old. You were stuck. Caring for her day by day, you depended on me to help you do it.

Your older daughter, Bernie, suffered from mental illness. Her behavior was a constant irritation. You could no more express affection to her than you could to me. I believed you felt guilty about that. Bernie's problems would never go away.

Mom, your life was next to hopeless. You were trapped. And you resented it.

When I thought of you today, I realized that I am not stuck. I have paid a high price for freedom. My divorce is one year old. My life is full of challenge, growth, fear and joy. My children are healthy. I don't need to be their perpetual caretaker. I am deeply grateful for that. And I don't take that blessing for granted.

The good news is I believe you are still with me. You will never leave me. And that is why I thought of you today, on you ninety-eighth birthday.

Today was a milestone for me. I took a financial risk. I used the internet to connect with a bank in Virginia, and, subsequently, I transferred my retirement account to them. I much prefer to bank in person, making direct contact rather than detached negotiations. But today I did what I needed to do, something that scared me.

As I transacted my business today, Mom, I thought of you. Somehow, I felt like you were giving me courage. I wanted to make a transaction with you, too.

Thanks, Mom, for caring in the only way you could. Thanks, for teaching me about faith. God is everything. And each of us must find God, the God of our understanding, in our own way. Your way was not my way. But you gave me the inclination to seek God. You illuminated the direction, if not the path, to a spirituality that pervades my being.

From all that our relationship was not, I release you. Forgive me for withdrawing from you. Help me to love my children and my grandchildren. Help me to give to others what I most craved from you.

I believe you are with me today. I hear you say, 'Take your Guardian Angel with you, Emmy!' That is your way of saying, 'Be safe. Go in peace.' I wish the same to you, Mom. At last, be at peace. Your struggles are over. I continue with mine. I am grateful for all that has brought me safely to this day. A new day. Your birthday. And mine. A new beginning for both of us."

Endnote: Today is May 14, 2023. I have shared my letter to you, Mom, with my 52-year-old daughter on Mother's Day.

Carol and I have bonded on a deep level. She is a warm and loving mother to Millie (19), Lachlan (17), and Quinn (13). At age 79, I am still learning to love unconditionally.

(Left to Right)) Grandma Em, Millie, Lachlan, Carol, and Quinn on Mother's Day, hiking on the Santa Fe Trail near Palmer Park, CO.

A Gardener's Perspective

When I recalled our home in Edgemont, I recalled that Mom maintained a smattering of houseplants. A couple red geraniums blossomed in the sunroom near my piano. Mom didn't fuss over her plants. All the attention they got was an occasional drink of water. Their firm stems reminded me of Mom's resilience. She never enhanced herself with cosmetics or jewelry, but she dressed neatly in public.

I thought of geraniums as "tough guys." They didn't require coddling. To prevent the plants from getting infected by decay, gardeners knew it was important to prune house plants by removing any leaves curling up or turning brown.

Cleaning house kept Mom on a weekly schedule of tasks. Defrosting the refrigerator on Friday, washing floors on Saturday, changing sheets on Monday was the routine. Neatness and cleanliness were priorities, Mom had little patience for her family when we did not pick up after ourselves. Of hearty German stock, my mother's roots grew deep in practicality and orderliness.

Chapter Thirteen
Colors of Grief

Greg received a bombshell phone call from Redfield in the Fall of 1992. Immediately, he called Charles and me. Emilie had been found on her bedroom floor. She had lived for the past three years in a group home. She had a big knot on her head, and she wouldn't wake up. No one could say with certainty what had happened. Had she fallen during the night on the way to the bathroom? Did she have an epileptic seizure? Or had another resident bashed her in an outburst of rage?

Although the cause of Emilie's fall was undetermined, the result was clear. Our sister was in a coma. She had been taken to a local hospital where she was being sustained on life support.

Shock and disbelief locked their jaws around my brothers and me as we waited for the next medical update. Several weeks vanished while all our thoughts were on Emilie. Finally, Greg got another call. All hope of Emilie's recovery was gone. The medical staff suggested that the time had come to discontinue life support and allow Emilie to die. Greg, Charles, and I were invited to come to the hospital for a last goodbye.

Numb, we clustered around the bedside of our comatose sister.

"We're here. We love you. Can you hear us?" I crooned as I caressed Emilie's arm.

Greg cautioned, "Maybe you shouldn't do that. You might upset her."

Unflinching, I continued, "I hope you don't hurt anywhere, Emilie. Can you wake up now?"

We waited, holding our collective breathe, but Emilie didn't stir. The breathing apparatus attached to her face continued to chug away with rhythmic, detached indifference.

Suddenly an urgent voice popped into my head.

Now's the time to use that holy oil you packed in your handbag. Anoint Emilie before the nurse disconnects her from oxygen!

Before my brothers and I were sent from Emilie's bedside to the waiting room, I removed a vial from my purse. Solemnly, I smeared the sign of Christ's cross on Emilie's forehead and hands. When I finished praying, my brothers and I quietly moved from the room.

We expected to get the, "She's gone" message within minutes after the life support was removed.

We waited.

We waited some more.

Finally, a doctor interrupted our silence. "Emilie is breathing on her own. Sometimes it takes a while when oxygen is removed."

Without brain waves or limb movement, Emilie continued to breath on her own, one gasp at a time—for six agonizing weeks!

During those ponderous days, as I waited for my twin sister to die, I reached for an eight-pack of crayons to express my grief. Those jumbo colors were waxy and strong, just what I needed to push depression and rage away from me.

Each day as I colored, I was amazed by the images that appeared on my pages.

I saved each drawing in a folder where it rested in my garage.

Thirty years passed before I examined those sketches again. Finally, I was ready to feel the intensity of my distress as I waited for Emilie to die. Crayons had told the story and held the enormity of my broken heart.

After each drawing, I had turned the page over and words had flowed from the core of my being. "I blessed Emilie last night, but I needed to repeat the ritual. I didn't have enough oil. I ran thin the second half of the cross. I felt awkward under the bright lights when a nurse walked by. I prayed that Emilie's spirit might be freed in peace. I will bless her again today."

I wrote a title on each picture I had drawn. "Set My Spirit Free".

I prayed aloud when I finished coloring and writing.

"Be free, Emilie, free of all pain. God, let me be free, too, from the need to understand. Let me find peace in being her twin sister."

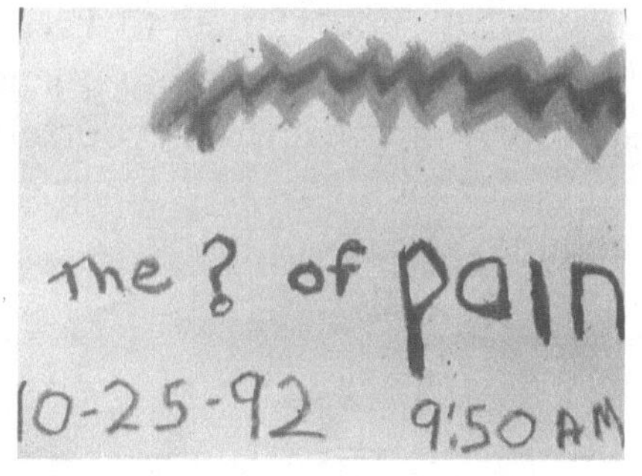

If there truly is a God of justice and mercy, I pray that Emilie will forever be free of pain!

I made another picture on October 27, entitled, *Emilie's Colors*. I did this one at 5:50 in the morning when I was back home in California. I had left Emilie in a coma in South Dakota.

On the back I wrote, "Waves of pain, small and tight, become more bearable as the crayon wears down. God, help me release jagged emotions. Let me look beyond myself again."

On a different day, I felt inspired to have a conversation with my pain and discover what lessons it might offer me.

Emma: What do you have to tell me, Pain? What am I to do with you?

Pain: Trust in the process. Take the next indicated step; listen to your gut.

Emma: Okay, I will call the hospital about Emilie. I will get a haircut. I will get some exercise.

Pain: You know by now...trust God. Keep on.

I continued to let words arise on the back of each drawing.

"Emilie, I carefully chose this box of eight crayons to put in your casket, expecting that we would bury you soon. But you did not die. You started to breathe on your own. Before the scheduled court hearing to mandate your removal from the respirator, you breathed by yourself. I'm left with a box of stubby crayons for me to use. My inner child celebrates your innocence, simplicity, and joy of being."

Emilie's colors told her story better than words could!

No update arrived from the hospital about Emilie's condition. Each morning, I awoke with the question, "Will this be the day Emilie dies?"

My stiff neck screamed with stress. I used Emilie's crayons to put my tension on paper. The sturdy wax willingly accepted the pressure I put on it.

On October 30, I sat at the desk in my home office. With a sketch pad and crayons at hand, I waited to see what image would appear—I didn't have to wait long.

The Flower of Death emerged spontaneously on my page. When I turned the drawing over, words described my dreamlike state of mind.

"I awoke with anxiety. Emilie was far away—there was an unreal quality about her existence. Now, more than ever, I acknowledged her energy in my soul. What was the next event…her death? Consciousness? Pneumonia? Infection? Moving to a nursing home?"

My body ached during a session with my internship supervisor. I let my grief flow. Flower of Death was in full bloom. I felt the reality of my aging and my eligibility for membership in the 55 Plus Group!

I knew my experience of loss would help me relate to my clients when I became a Marriage and Family Therapist.

Greg, the designated family contact, got the dreaded phone call from Redfield on December 5th. "Emilie has stopped breathing," the caller reported. One short statement ended our long vigil. It seemed like we had been holding our breath for six weeks, waiting for Emilie to take that one final gasp.

The following days brought a blizzard of activities through which we plowed. Preparing for the wake at Osheim Catron Funeral Home, Rose and I chose Emilie's burial garments. Comfortable pull-on slacks with a floral cotton smock were what she had always worn.

On December 9th, the funeral Mass was celebrated at Blessed Sacrament Church. This was where the Kopriva family worshiped in Rapid City. One of the hymns I picked for the liturgy was "Come unto Me" written by Bob Hurd. I knew that God treasured Emilie just as she was. She hadn't spoken wise words or accomplish great things. Emilie mattered despite achievements.

Greg and I read passages from the Bible during the liturgy. Proclaiming God's Word eased our burdened spirit, a brief respite from our grief.

Since we had a family burial plot in Edgemont, we headed there after the Mass. Emilie was transported by hearse the ninety miles to our hometown. She had spent the first 17 years of her life in the big house on Second Ave. Now she was finally returning home.

Greg, Charles, and I followed behind in the procession, hovering guardian angels.

Dry weeds and sharp stones covered the rustic cemetery where we brought Emilie to join Mom and Daddy. The city water tower watched over us knowingly on that Wednesday afternoon. Stillness was joined by a gust of wind as Father Ray intoned a final blessing over the casket. The stark hilltop was all-too-familiar terrain. Only seven months had passed since we had accompanied Mom to this destination. Daddy had been resting here for 27 years, since 1967.

I wished life had been gentler and softer for my family. Instead, it had been as harsh as this rugged knoll where we left Emilie.

After the final graveside rite, my brothers and I departed the cemetery with lead-heavy hearts. We decided to grab a bite of comfort food at the Fresh Start Truck Stop, the only eatery in town. We weren't hungry, but we needed to take some time to process these past weeks.

When we first sat down at the table, no one wanted to talk for several minutes. How could words contain the sadness throbbing inside us?

In Memory Of

Emilie Kopriva

August 5, 1943 December 5, 1992

CHRISTIAN WAKE SERVICE
Osheim-Catron Funeral Home
Rapid City, South Dakota
Tuesday, December 8, 1992 7:00 p.m.

MASS OF CHRISTIAN BURIAL
Blessed Sacrament Church
Rapid City, South Dakota
Wednesday, December 9, 1992 9:00 a.m.

CELEBRANT
Rev. Raymond Deisch

MUSIC BY
Blessed Sacrament Ladies Choir

PALLBEARERS
Dr. Gregory J. Kopriva Dr. Charles J. Kopriva
Charles A. Kopriva Lawrence E. Kopriva

INTERMENT
Edgemont Cemetery
Edgemont, South Dakota

One small memorial card commemorated the tragic life of my twin sister.

Unexpectedly, I remembered when Jesus told his followers from the cross on Calvary that his work was finished. (John 19:30). At last, Emilie's Earthly mission was over.

Is it really finished? Can I let go now of responsibility? Is it okay to feel relief at last?

Finally, my brothers and I allowed words to seep out of us. We pooled stories about the folks who used to fill the *Locals* of the Edgemont Tribune.

As we chatted, I noticed a cloud of depression was enveloping me. I thought of our sister Bernie, who resided in senior living in Minnesota. We had not encouraged her to come to Emilie's funeral. She had not pressed us to attend. She didn't have a car. No family member wanted to drive a dozen hours in winter snow to bring her to the memorial service.

What was most difficult to deal with about Bernie was not the mileage that separated us or the icy roads. It was the emotional inferno that exploded whenever all of us were together.

Long ago, we had stopped including Bernie in family gatherings. We didn't want to be brought down by her irascibility. Anger clung to her like a piece of lint to a black coat. We knew that any family reunion would eventually escalate into a Vesuvius of rage.

For certain, no one was up for Bernie's outburst of anger as we buried Emilie.

After an hour of reminiscing at the restaurant, my brothers and I trudged through the truck-stop parking lot. We gassed up the Olds for the trip back to Rapid City, SD. Laden with moisture, the dark clouds felt like our unshed tears.

We rode past the cemetery on the outskirts of town. As we traveled down the highway, I recalled the funeral that morning.

Don't Tell!

Right after Mass, nobody was looking.

I slipped a brand new eight-pack of crayons into the casket. Before the lid was closed for the last time, I fervently prayed. "Enjoy your colors, Emilie. Have fun scribbling on the walls of heaven. Rest in peace, my sister! Color to your heart's content."

A Gardener's Perspective

Dressed in vivid colors, primroses taught me that Creator God was playful. Growing in both shaded and sunny spots, this edible and medicinal herb flirted boldly in my garden.

Primroses were associated with fairies that floated languidly through flower beds. Gazing at this plant brought me to a state of wonder. Calming and soothing, the primrose was used by folks seeking to doze, to escape pain. My garden was a sanctuary for sleepy dreams.

Emilie observed what was going on around her. She had no tasks to perform. Curious eyes gazed at her. Unable to use words, her quiet message was unspoken. She colored on walls like primroses colored gardens. Fairies danced in delight.

Chapter Fourteen
Gramp

I often thought of my paternal grandfather, Charles Joseph Kopriva. Each remembrance was a gift, wrapped in tenderness and tied with a bow of love. To me and my siblings, he was fondly known as *Gramp*. My grandfather resided at the house on Second Ave. during my toddler years. After that, he farmed a swatch of land and sold produce to townspeople until his death in 1957. How Gramp arrived at our house was a story from long ago and far away in Czechoslovakia.

Examining ancestorial roots, I found Gramp's father, Karel Kopriva, was born in 1826, and his mother, Theresa Novak, ten years later. The family arrived at Ellis Island in 1862 and settled in Minnesota. Gramp was born on November 1, 1872 in New Prague, Le Sueur County.

Gramp with his bride, Katherine Jindra

My grandpa was twenty-four years old when he married Katherine Jindra on April 15, 1896 at Saint Stanislaus Church in Saint Paul. They raised two daughters, Alice and Ruth, and four sons,

Richard, Marcus, Charles, and my father, Lawrence, who arrived in 1899.

According to my Aunt Alice, Gramp was a successful general store owner in Bowbells, North Dakota. One night the family home burned to the ground because the coal stove was left unattended. No one died that night, but the family was left in dire financial straits. Gramp gave up the mercantile business. He headed out with his brothers to develop nearby land, available by the Homestead Act. When dry weather caused crops to fail, Gramp was forced to abandon the farm.

Details of the Kopriva story were as scrambled as eggs in a breakfast omelet. By the time I began to interview elderly relatives in 1984, memories of the *old days* were dim. The sequence of events was vague, presenting more questions than answers.

Gramp's wife, Katherine, died at age fifty-three, on August 11, 1927 (fifteen years before my birth). Her death certificate identified her cause of death as cardiac disease, but her children said she died of a broken heart due to the family downturn. She was buried in the Kopriva plot at Calvary Cemetery in Saint Paul, the area where the family had first settled in America.

After his wife died, Gramp moved from North Dakota back to Minnesota with his daughter, Alice. During the last decades of his life, Gramp resided with his son Lawrence and family in South Dakota. That's how my grandfather came into my life.

As I wrote in 2024, my two living siblings, Greg and Charles helped me iron out the wrinkles in the fraying narrative. One sobering fact was clear, the Koprivas had come on hard times in North Dakota. Tragedy had pulled them from financial success to heart-breaking poverty, long before my twin sister and I joined the family.

In 1943, twins arrived for Emma and Lawrence. The dark cloud of misfortune continued. Mom had been on the brink of death for three weeks. Details of her decline were sketchy. Some recalled she had a pulmonary embolism and immediately went into a coma after giving birth.

The household was distracted by grief. In the chaos, Gramp stepped up to choose names for the newborns. For me, he picked Emma, after my mother, followed by Katherine after his deceased wife. I never knew why Gramp named my twin Emilie.

Because I was named after a grandma I had never met, I was curious in adult years, to learn about her. My research fascinated me. Katherine Jindra was born in1874. Her father, Winislaw Jindra, was born in Bohemia in 1844. He earned a living as a shoemaker.

My family tree had lured me to dusty events from generations past. Eventually, the spotlight refocused on the folks living in the Edgemont house during my younger days. Gramp loomed large in my memories of childhood.

My grandfather resided in our household on Second Avenue until 1948. I was five years old when he relocated to a couple acres across the street and down the hill. *The Place*, as Gramp called it, was a one room shack where he lived with no indoor plumbing.

With a youngster's wide eyes and open ears, I took in all the sights, sounds, and smells of Gramp's farm. For me, the scariest spot on The Place was a root cellar. I kept my distance from rattlesnakes and rats.

During the summer, the cellar was as cool as a refrigerator. Sacks of sweet corn waited for my brother there. Everyone in town knew Charlie from his bicycle deliveries. Townspeople enjoyed the aroma of roasting ears of corn for supper. Gramp did a flourishing business.

Scenes from the Gramp Years were scattered randomly on my memory screen. Like the frolicking youngsters we had been, our adventures spilled over with energy.

Gramp rested in the heavy oak rocker in our living room, contentedly puffing on his pipe. He handed Greg ten cents in change.

“Run uptown and grab the latest edition of the Denver Post. Keep the change.”

Loose pennies jingling in his pocket, Greg rushed to Highley’s Drug Store to select his favorite candy before heading home with the newspaper.

Gramp sat at the foot of the dining table, opposite Daddy at the head.

Because I was next to him, I had a bird’s eye view when Gramp removed his dentures.

He placed them carefully near his plate.

Oh, God, please don’t let me puke!

Averting my eves in revulsion when those pink-gummed dentures showed up, I tried my best to think about something else. Gulping down my food, I escaped from the dinner table like a prisoner fleeing for her life.

I loved going to church, even as a young girl.

Don't Tell!

While the rest of the family went to eight o'clock Mass on Sunday morning, my job was to stay at home and supervise Emilie. This arrangement allowed me to attended Mass a couple hours later by myself, and I liked that. I felt comforted by the predictable rituals and chants of the liturgy.

If I was at Linda's house on Sunday evening, I would rush away. Chatter with my friend didn't grab me like services at Saint James did. It was not obligation or parental pressure that brought me to church, although that certainly influenced me. The frosting on the cake of church attendance was seeing my Gramp in his habitual spot. The back pew, across the center aisle was where he always settled.

Gramp would already be in his pew when I arrived. He was never late for church. Seeing my grandfather always pleased me, even though I didn't know what to say to him.

Shy little girls didn't talk much.

When Gramp had moved from our house to his own residence, I didn't see him every day anymore. That made church encounters with him more special, whether the service was Sunday Mass, Benediction, or Stations of the Cross. I always sat in my spot near him, where I could steal a glance at Gramp, the rosary beads moving steadily between his fingers. I felt a bond with him, knowing that we both found comfort in our faith. God was part of who we were, like a gentle hymn we hummed together, my grandfather and me.

Gramp was in my life for only a short time, from my birth in 1943 until his death in 1957.

He stayed at the Edgemont house until I was five.

While at our house, Gramp shared the north bedroom upstairs with my brother.

Greg was a skinny kid. On the other hand, Gramp was portly, causing the bed to sag toward the floor on his side. Greg would roll downhill into Gramp's back during the night. It didn't take long for Gramp to find a 2' X 4' to put down the center of the bed. From then on, both sleepers co-existed comfortably on the same mattress. No doubt about it, our Gramp was a practical man.

Gramp was safe and kind. He never yelled at me.

"Get something you really like, maybe some new socks," Gramp said as he handed me a birthday card with a crisp dollar bill inside.

"Thanks, Gramp," I responded shyly.

Socks are boring. What can I get instead with my money?

A dollar was a fortune in the eyes of a six-year-old in 1949. I soon decided to hang onto my cash until I found something exciting to spend it on. Although I was tempted to blow my money on dime- store candy, I kept it for months. It was almost Easter when, in the window of Gifford's Variety, I spied a toy bank, Peter Rabbit. He was wearing brown-rimmed glasses and farmer duds just like Gramp's. I knew immediately that Peter Rabbit was worth every penny of my life savings.

Eagerly I surrendered my dollar to the clerk behind the counter at the dime store.

It doesn't matter that I won't have any coins left to put in my new bank.

Peter Rabbit greeted me with a hug whenever I spotted him on my bedroom dresser.

Years rushed me from childhood into adulthood.

Steadfast, Peter Rabbit waited for me.

He waited until I came home from college.

He was there when I returned with my new family from Los Angeles.

Life chugged on like a determined train.

In 1987, my sister-in-law, Rose and I cleared everything out the Edgemont house, so it could be put up for sale. Boxing up clothes, dishes, and Christmas decorations was a sweaty task in the July attic that had no air conditioning. Sorting through dusty cardboard boxes was like doing a life review, not just of events of my generation, but of decades before. The nut cups from my mother's bridal shower in 1929 were saturated with nostalgia as were the tender love letters my parents exchanged during their courtship. Tears mingled with perspiration as I worked in the stifling attic where time stood still.

Discerning what to save and what to toss away was a soul-searching process for me. As a retired English teacher, I recalled a practical grammar rule to avoid excessive use of commas, "When in doubt, throw it out."

Woefully, I admitted that in my California home I had not a single empty closet or a vacant shelf where I could store childhood mementos. Common Sense advised me not to collect memorabilia if I had nowhere to display it. When I spotted Peter Rabbit, waiting on my dresser, I thought, "In the busy life of a forty-five-year-old woman there is no space for a kid's plastic rabbit bank." I realized that neither of my teenagers, caught up in peer relationships and high school activities, would be interested in having a plastic bank that their mom once cherished. A sob escaping my throat, I placed Peter Rabbit in a box of rummage sale donations.

Gramp's fingerprints were smudged all over our lives.

When my 16-year-old brother, Charles, wanted to buy a 1929 Model A pickup, Gramp helped him with the finances. All the girls at Edgemont High admired Charlie, chugging down the street in his dilapidated jalopy. Gramp knew what it was to be young and to have dreams.

A lady named Clara brought a glimmer of romance into Gramp's life at a time of family tragedy. When Emilie and I were born, Mom had an undiagnosed medical emergency, on the verge of death. When Mom finally returned home after weeks in a coma, she was in no shape to run the household or to tend to newborn twins much less three older kids. To help out, Mom's 19-year-old sister, Marie, came from the family farm in Nenzel, Nebraska. Marie stayed only a few weeks.

Then a long-term caregiver, Mrs. Clara Sweeney, was hired. She was a widow who owned a house in Cottonwood, on the outskirts of Edgemont, near the railroad tracks. I have no personal memory of this helper. However, Clara made a remarkable impression on my grandfather.

Gramp, a widower for 16 years, soon became *sweet* on the capable widow, a daily presence in the Kopriva household.

Greg was 14 years old when Mrs. Sweeney came on the family scene. One day, after school, Greg came into the kitchen just in time to catch Gramp kissing Mrs. Sweeney. Quickly, secret romance spread through the family. Gramp wanted to marry the kindly widow, Clara, but his kids opposed the bond.

Conflict spread among Gramp's children. Some believed Gramp would betray their mother by remarrying. My father was in that camp. He was only 28 when his beloved mother had passed away in 1927. When the budding love story was discovered, Mrs. Sweeney abruptly departed from the Kopriva household. Mom was left on her own to manage the home and family as best she could. As for Gramp, thoughts of remarriage were quashed forever.

I don't know what happened to Mrs. Sweeney after she stopped working for our family. Did she continued to live in Cottonwood on the other side of the train track?

The Gramp Years ended all too soon, bringing my childhood escapades to an abrupt stop. Although Gramp had heart problems for years, it was stomach cancer that finally claimed him. I was 13 when he was taken to the nearest hospital in Hot Springs for exploratory surgery. No remedy was available to save his life. During his final two weeks, his five adult children grieved at his bedside.

All the relatives packed into the Edgemont house. As usual, my job was to help Mom clean and care for Emilie. Aunt Alice labeled me, *The Little Gold Dust Twin.* I got the idea she was concerned about my religious upbringing and general care.

She asked, "Do you ever pray?" I replied shyly, "Yes." I felt embarrassed, like she thought I was a heathen. Beyond that, I sensed her genuine concern for me, a child shouldering grown-up responsibility.

After Daddy finished his day's work on the Tribune, he would drive 26 miles each evening to see Gramp. I stayed home with Emilie every night, my routine job, while the rest of the family made the hospital visit.

After ten days, Aunt Alice asked, "Shouldn't Emmy be allowed to see Gramp, too?"

As we made our way to Hot Springs that evening, I was grateful to be recognized as part of the family…not just a housemaid.

No words described the scene that awaited me at the hospital.

Aways timid, I didn't "break down" when I reached for the hand of my unconscious grandfather, lying still in the bed. I was too late to talk to him, but I was grateful to touch him one more time.

"*Gramp, I miss you!*"

Uncles and aunts, in loud voices, recounted tales of the Bowbells Mercantile Store. Bursts of laughter erupted in our crowded living room, as I helped Mom prepare trays of food in the kitchen.

With a jolt, I asked myself, "Where's Gramp? Someone should run down the hill to get him, so he won't miss out!"

In an instant, cold reality replied, "Gramp's dead. He won't be coming to this party."

Early the next morning, I watched as his casket was loaded on the freight train. Our father's heavy footsteps headed to the passenger car to accompany Gramp on the final journey.

Calvary Cemetery in Saint Paul was a spot I never visited. Gramp has rested there for sixty-seven years.

I still can hear the Burlington chugging down the tracks in the morning sun, taking my grandfather far away.

Truth was, Gramp never left.

He remained…as close as my own heartbeat.

In Memory of
CHARLES JOSEPH KOPRIVA, SR.
November 1, 1872 - February 26, 1957
Services
ST. JAMES CATHOLIC CHURCH
Edgemont, S. Dak.
9:30 A. M. Saturday, March 2, 1957
Officiating Clergyman
MSGR. C. N. BIEVER
Rosary, Friday, 8 p. m.
McColley Chapel
Casket Bearers
George Tupper, Jack Kane, E. M. Nielsen, Philip Roller, Roy Hudson, Ivan Barkley.
Honorary Pallbearers
J. M. Tucker, Charles Nightengale, Richard Pfister, Marvin Cummings, Joe Bayer, Don Foxhoven.
Place of Interment
Calvary Cemetery
Saint Paul, Minn.

Gramp's memorial flyer in 1957

In 1955, I was 12 years old and Gramp, seated between my parents, was 83.

A Gardener's Perspective

From the time I was five years old, Gramp lived on The Place, a shack on a couple acres of land, off the main drag in Edgemont. Two goats in the barn provided milk for my twin sister's delicate stomach. Chickens, fluttering about the smelly henhouse, produced fresh eggs for local customers. Geese wandered around the paddock as if they owned the farm. On the walls of the shed, Fall River County Fair Blue Ribbons testified to the juicy roasted ears of corn and succulent tomatoes Gramp raised on his land.

Since I moved from Los Angeles to Colorado Springs in 2011, I have savored eating breakfast in my backyard in the summer. Joined by squirrels scampering atop the fence, doves cooing in the aspens, and spiders webbing on lawn chairs, I was at peace. I have discovered My Place, in the garden, with my God and with my Gramp.

Chapter Fifteen
Tribute to Rose

Rose, my sister-in-law for nearly 53 years, was dying! I had no time to edit or polish my words. I just had to get a message to her as fast as I could. Her life was running out, like water through a sieve. My heart was exploding with unspoken feelings. By postal service, the message wouldn't arrive before she died.

Grabbing my cell phone, I blurted to my nephew, Larry, in Rapid City, "Go open the letter I just *emailed* to you! Someone must read it to your mom next time she's awake. Before it's too late—she's got to know!"

Rose died four days after I fired off my final message to her.

A week later, Greg asked me to read that hurried email at Rose's wake.

I hesitated for only a moment before I somberly replied, "Yes."

Could I share with the world intimate memories, written just for Rose? What if I burst into tears in front of the whole church?

Deep inside, I knew I could read my message aloud. After all, I was an expert at stuffing my feelings. I knew how to seem calm when I was nervous and how to act courageous when I was scared.

When I felt uncertain about sharing the email, I reassured myself.

You've got this. You will read it for Rose. After all, she did so much for you!

The evening of the wake arrived. Sheer determination empowered me, like hot steam. I headed to the microphone to pour out my heart before the congregation. In that moment, I was "The Little Engine that Could," from a childhood storybook.

When I finished reading, moments later, I returned to my seat in the pew.

I read the whole thing, without a tear or a tremor. She cared for me, and I cared for her—not in a sentimental way, but with simple kindness.

I wrote this remembrance thirteen years after that vigil service. It was July 2023. I was eager to share my final words to Rose because I want others to know her the way I did. The tears that I had held back at the wake in 2010 burst from me as I wrote, refusing to be contained a day longer. Sobs, like bullet points, accentuate the list of specific occasions when Rose helped me. I did not tamper with the words of the original farewell message to the woman who saved my life. A portrait of my sister-in-law was created with lasting gratitude.

July 17, 2010

Dear Rose,

Since I can't be present with you now as you are dying, I am writing to thank you for the many ways you touched my life. You might be embarrassed to mention these things yourself, but they meant so much to me. You always looked out for me, especially when no one else was looking. I was thirteen when you came into our family. You could see us with an objectivity we did not have. And you cared for all of us by your thoughtfulness and hard work.

Whenever your family came to dinner at our house in Edgemont, you cleaned the kitchen and the refrigerator, removing rancid lard and stale food. You came into chaos, and you left order. These were tasks meant for me, jobs that felt overwhelming to a child. But you helped in every way you could.

On Sundays, you insisted on including me in your family outings. You knew I needed to get away. You were aware that Mom didn't pay attention to me, and you tried to fill the gap.

When Daddy was in the throes of alcoholism, you cooked breakfast for him at the duplex in Edgemont and helped him to reach sobriety.

You never forgot my birthday when I was a schoolgirl. I loved clothes, and you would let me pick from the catalogue a dress I preferred. In those days, dresses sold for $3.99 or $4.99. Sometimes you gave me hand-me-downs, a skirt, blouse, or jacket you wore in college. I still remember some of the clothes. But most of all, I remember that you cared.

I babysat your children. They were like little sisters and brothers to me. You paid me money for this, so I could buy film for my camera.

You looked after Bernie, taking the initiative for her safety. This meant you drove or flew across the country to get her when her life was in danger. You left your own kids at home to do what needed to be done.

You helped the family to see that home care was not meeting Emilie's needs, and you initiated steps to get her into a residential facility. If it hadn't been for you, I, as the "Well Twin," would have been expected to give my life to Emilie's care. I have you to thank that I was allowed to attend college and to have a life of my own. Due to your persistence, Emilie entered Redfield State Hospital just when I was ready to enter college. You visited Emilie whenever your family was anywhere near Redfield. This was a sad visit, but you did not avoid it. You never turned your back on family.

When I graduated from high school in 1961, it was you who bought me suitcases, bedding, and dishes to send me off into the world of higher education. Having never been away from home, I was insecure and homesick that first year at USD. You sent homemade cookies, a teddy bear, and a trench coat. A care package from home helped me cope with a bigger world beyond Edgemont, South Dakota.

When I came home from college during holidays, you let me take your kids out to lunch and to the movies. Being Auntie Em has always been a tender joy.

Because I didn't have a car, you would drive me to the Mountain View Care Center to visit Mom while I was in town. Those visits were stilted and painful, but you did your best to help Mom and me to connect. I felt inspired to bless Mom on one of my visits. I had always been guarded about sharing my spiritual self with my mother. Despite that, I hesitantly took a vial of oil from my purse. Bernie was with me the day I asked Mom if I could bless her. Mom readily agreed. Oil was still smeared on my fingers when Bernie asked me for a blessing, too. I was stunned when Bernie immediately asked if she could bless me, and she did.

Next thing I knew, when you got back to your house that day, Rose, Bernie blurted out what had just happened in Mom's room. I felt embarrassed to hear Bernie spill out the whole story. But do you remember what happened next, Rose? In a sudden moment of inspiration, I asked if I could bless you and Greg! And you said, "Yes." So, I prayed with the two of you, also. I am so grateful for that day whenever I think about it. You blessed me in so many ways. I am glad you let me bless you, too.

You knew I had lived a cloistered life with little social interaction with my peers during high school. The summer of 1967, before my August wedding, you wanted me to meet your children's tennis coach, to expand my social world. I was hardly ready for marriage. You must have sensed that. You were right.

When I planned my wedding, you encouraged Mom to pay for the wedding luncheon at the Embers. And, years later at Christmas, it was you who planted the seed that Mom might send money for Christmas gifts for my family. You helped Mom be a mom.

At your fiftieth wedding anniversary celebration, Charles and I decided to publicly say a few words to thank you, Rose, for all you have done for our family. The spontaneity of my comments before the community surprised me when I stated, "You were like a mother to me." The truth just slipped out. I was stunned. You looked at me and nodded your head. How readily and openly you acknowledged our relationship.

As a young wife and mother, when I was facing a decision, I used to ask myself, "What would Rose do?" You were a role model for sensible, practical, dedicated love in action—an example I could trust.

I am so grateful for those vacations you spent in Green Valley, Arizona. How good it was for you and Greg to relax and to enjoy your family away from frigid South Dakota winters. Thanks for including Charles and me sometimes.

As I look back on your life, I hope you nod with recognition and satisfaction and say, "Yes, for this I came." Your coming into our lives has forever changed us all. Thank you, Rose. With love and prayers,

Emmy

Rose's health had been declining for several years. The whole family witnessed death wrestling with her. As I look back, I ponder why I didn't go in person to her bedside. The voice in my head had an immediate answer.

"She's not really your mom. You're not really one of her chicks. You would only be in the way. Besides, what would you say to her? You don't know how to talk about gushy stuff. It's better to stand back. Don't interrupt the privacy due to her family in her dying moments."

The timid, undeserving girl I knew from childhood convinced me to watch Rose's dying from afar, at my home in Los Angeles. After revealing my whole self in that naked email, I wanted to hide. At the same time, I wanted to be part of the family and to honor Rose.

I waited and waited some more for a response to my email.

Did Rose get my message? Did she understand? What happened?

I agonized.

The questioning voice I heard in my head was my own. Three days of waiting oozed by before I called my niece, Linda, in Rapid City. I could wait no longer!

What had happened with my email?

I waited forever, holding my breath before I picked up the phone.

Linda and Mary poured out the story. Halted by tears, my precious nieces, who were like little sisters to me, took turns telling the narrative.

Rose had been sleeping frequently as death pressed down on her tired body like a heavy quilt. During one of her awake moments after a dose of pain medication, the girls gently guided her from the bedroom and settled her in her favorite armchair in the living room. They read my email, phrase by phrase, and Rose listened attentively. Occasionally, she interrupted her daughters and hoarsely interjected comments.

"She never knew how special she was. Many times, she was the only one I could count on."

There were long pauses, like notes held in a musical score. When Rose would gasp for breath, Linda wrote down her mother's words.

Mary would soothe her mom when weakness overcame her.

Then the rhythm of reading, listening, and commenting continued once more.

"I'm amazed she turned out so well. I am so proud of her!"

Fatigued by being out of bed, Rose dozed off, then the pattern would continue in the same rhythm.

"I felt bad she didn't have a warm coat in Edgemont."

A new verse arising in her lyrics, Rose carried on down Memory Lane.

"Almost every day, she walked to the hospital to see Daddy."

Rose was ready to nod off in sleep by the time Mary stopped reading my farewell message. Then she drowsily whispered the words I will cherish forever.

"Emmy was worth every little bit of it!"

Moved by Rose's response to my email, I made a framed poster of her last words to me so I could ponder them frequently, especially in hard times. I owed my life to my sister-in-law. She believed in me long before I believed in myself.

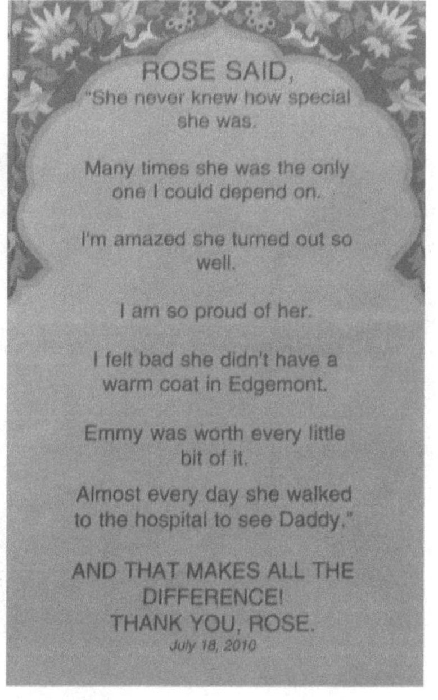

As a young girl growing up, I always wanted to be on my best behavior around my sister-in-law. Because she believed in me, I never wanted to disappoint her. Years later, when I was a young woman with children of my own, I felt clueless about how to mother. I watched closely as Rose guided her children. Sometimes she gave me parenting tips, but mostly she taught by example. When my five-year-old daughter, Carol, hummed during dinner, Rose chided gently, "That's not what we do at the table."

Sorrow, not despair, formed Rose into the tender woman she was, able to help others in their darkest moments. Her father, a Missouri farmer, had worked doubly hard in his fields to compensate for a painful bone disorder. His twisted knee and gimpy leg slowed him down.

Rose was 22 when tragedy jolted the Eccher family. Her older brother, Warren, was killed on his motorcycle when a drunk driver smashed into him on a country hillside.

My sister-in-law, Rose Kopriva, always believed in my right to have a life of my own. Rose (on the left) was 71 and I was 56 in this photo taken in 1999. She and Greg traveled to California to bolster me during a turbulent divorce. Rose encouraged me to do what I needed to do after 31 years of marriage.

I was 13 *w*hen Rose married my brother Greg in 1956. She hadn't met any of our clan during their courtship. Greg never talked about the dark side of our family, only of our accomplishments. Shame stopped him from disclosing our pain. Our father was an alcoholic. Our mother was emotionally unstable. One sister was mentally ill, another mentally retarded. "Why didn't you tell Rose what our family was really like before you married her?" I asked. Greg replied pensively, "It was too sad!"

When Rose said, "I do," on her wedding day, it was without full knowledge our family situation.

Would Rose have joined such a troubled family had she known?

An Army nurse with a degree in psychology, Rose could identify emotional illness when she spotted it. She urged our parents to institutionalize Emilie for adequate care. In the 1980's, when Redfield pressured the Kopriva family to move Emilie to a less restrictive environment, Rose foresaw danger. Defenseless Emilie needed close supervision to protect her from violent residents.

Greg relied on Rose's practical wisdom to assist him in his professional office. Rose's intuition and people skills shined when it came time to hire a new dental assistant. She had a knack for choosing top-notch staff and for bookkeeping, too.

Rose managed family matters with kindness and clarity.

Daddy was hospitalized the summer of 1967. I was on break after my second year of teaching French in Cheyenne, Wyoming.

Rose initiated the idea that I sit by Daddy's bedside to keep him company. He required an advocate, since he could hardly speak. I became my father's voice.

Those days at Saint John's Hospital were unforgettable. I would peddle my bike five miles each morning to be his Guardian Angel. His cruel bedsores refused to heal. Peaceful rest came only with medication.

Squirming with awkwardness, I didn't know how to make conversation with my father. I didn't really know him. My role in the family had been to help Mom. My older siblings, Daddy's helpers, communicated easily with him.

Time passed slowly at Saint John's.

My uncomfortable presence was all I could give Daddy in his final days.

Rose understood.

Me too.

Each day at the hospital, I had a ring-side seat to my father's dying.

I showed up because I loved Rose.

I loved my father, too.

While Daddy napped in the afternoon, I hasten away from his bedside. The dress shops of downtown Rapid City beckoned.

For my wedding to James Lee, which was only a month away, I needed a special gown. Time was running short.

I was planning a wedding and preparing for a funeral at the same time.

When the big day came, August 12, my father wasn't strong enough to attend the ceremony. My new husband and I, fresh from our vow-speaking at Blessed Sacrament Church, visited my father. He had been moved to a care facility. Rooted in a wheelchair, Daddy handed us a wedding card. Signed with his labored, palsied hand, that treasure became one my most precious mementos. Daddy was present on our wedding day in the only way he could be.

Fifty-six years later, I still cherished his nuptial blessing.

Rose taught me that our presence was the best gift we had to offer. She was always present in our family's big moments.

When I was still single, I was more readily available to travel than my married siblings were. Rose would count on me to be collected and patient when disaster erupted. She sent me on several family missions.

Once in the 1960's, at Rose's direction, I took the Greyhound to Kemmerer, Wyoming to check up on my older sister. Bernie was barely surviving as a dishwasher at a restaurant.

In 1983, I turned up in Aberdeen, South Dakota. My job was to keep vigil with my twin sister as she recovered from a hysterectomy.

Another time, Rose sent me to Florida. My job was getting Daddy and Mom safely home following Daddy's Parkinsons evaluation.

My brother, Charles, a medical student, had gone before me to consult with medical experts.

Rose was the one who pulled us together in hard times. Often, she and Greg had to leave their small children with a babysitter to do what needed to be done for our family. Greg had to close his dental office to tend to family matters.

No one quibbled with Rose about stepping up to help. She led by her example of practical, steadfast love. We all wanted to do our part. We always respected Rose's leadership during crises.

Rose and Greg's children, Linda, Jim, Mary, Charles, and Larry had always been like brothers and sisters to me. We shared our struggles and our victories. They would seek my advice in rough times. Supporting my nieces and nephews was my way to give back to Rose. I guided and cherished her family in the same way that she had helped me. Being "Auntie Em" was a privilege.

Rose whole-heartedly served her country as a surgical nurse in Austria, Italy, and Germany. In 1956, she became a Captain in the Army at the age of 28, at Fort Knox, KY. In 2023, I visited her gravesite to thank her once again for mothering me.

When she died, her family chose Micah 6:8 for her memorial verse. Rose's code of ethics was summarized in these words, "Act justly, love mercy, walk humbly with your God." That's how Rose lived.

A few weeks before her death on July 23, 2010, Rose reflected in her journal about her marriage to my brother.

"We have had many problems, worries, and struggles over the years (almost 53), but our love together, and the love, caring and help from family and friends, and our faith in God has sustained us. We are very thankful to all who have helped us along the way. Hard work, education, healthy living, faith in God, and love and respect for others is the way to peace and a good life."

Rose and Greg were married at Fort Knox, KY on December 28, 1956. Their children honored them with a 50th anniversary celebration.

Greg, almost 93 years old, mourns his beloved wife of nearly 53 years at the Black Hills National Cemetery near Sturgis, SD, September 2023.

A Gardener's Perspective

In ancient Egypt, iris blossoms were sacred, a symbol of power, wisdom, faith, and valor. No wonder I thought of my sister-in-law whenever I gazed on these stately flowers.

Rose carried herself with dignity, never losing control of her emotions or her values. She stood tall, not questioning her purpose or anyone else's. As a spouse, a mother, a sister-in-law, Rose was confident in her moral code. By example, she modeled how to act justly, to love mercy, and to walk humbly with God.

The vivid colors of iris blossoms reminded me of the curly red hair, freckles, and green eyes that set Rose apart in unique beauty. She chose to direct her attention to her family or to her garden rather than to herself. Comfortable in her own skin, Rose intuitively knew how to respect herself and to appreciate others.

I was grateful that Rose saw me as more than a caregiver. She knew me as a person in my own right, not just one of the twins. For the good of the whole family, Rose encouraged my parents to institutionalize Emilie, allowing me to have a life of my own. She stands tall as an iris at the center of my Garden of Memories.

Chapter Sixteen
Farewell, Bernie!

Although my brothers (Greg and Charles) were experienced writers for the family newspaper, they were not eager to write an obituary for Bernie. Looking back, I couldn't blame them. Who jumped at the chance to write an obit, especially when the deceased lived a life marred by tragedy? How did a writer protect family secrets, and yet honor a deceased sister? No one wanted to touch Bernie's story. Her funeral was just a couple weeks away. The deadline to submit an obituary to the hometown newspaper and to the regional paper was right now.

Funeral planning seemed to come under the heading of "Women's Work" in our family. Preparing for a memorial service was no fun for anyone. Gathering photos for a video, writing an obituary, picking out a casket were tasks my brothers gladly left to me. Irritation rose up from within me like smoke from a bonfire.

Why would I expect life-long gender roles to be any different now that I'm 79? Why can't my brothers help me? I hate this situation as much as they do!

Reluctantly, I opened my Mac. I began to write the summary of my sister's life, her memorial obituary. The words seemed eager to pour out a story that needed to be told.

In one hour, I was finished writing a sanitized narrative, bleached clean from soiled misery and neatly organized like fresh laundry. My glimpse hardly did justice to the 90 years Bernie had lived. It failed to mention that my sister had been institutionalized six times for mental illness. Only after she escaped from a locked hospital had she gained a semblance of freedom. Otherwise, she might have spent 60 years confined.

I'm so proud of you, Bernie! Taking your freedom into your own hands!

Life outside the hospital had been an uphill climb for a woman restricted by depression and anxiety. Only our immediate family knew the full extent of Bernie's challenges. As the reluctant writer of her obituary, I was determined not to disclose all her troubles. Only a well-refined version of her life would hit the newspaper.

MEMORIAL OBITUARY FOR
ANGELA BERNADETTE KOPRIVA
(1932-2022)

Angela Bernadette Kopriva, 90, Tracy, MN, passed away Tuesday, July 19, 2022, at Hospice House in Slayton, MN. She was the daughter of Lawrence Karl Kopriva and Emma Kopriva, long-time residents of Edgemont, SD.

Bernie was born March 11, 1932, in Cody, Nebraska. She grew up in Waukesha, WI for seven years until the family settled in Edgemont in 1939. Following graduation from Edgemont High School, Bernie attended Saint Mary's College in Omaha, NE, for secretarial training. Returning to Edgemont, Bernie worked as a typesetter for her father, Lawrence, editor and publisher of The Edgemont Tribune.

In 1964, Bernie settled in Marshall, MN, which became her home until 2016.

She was an active member of Divine Redeemer Catholic Church. Declining health caused Bernie to move to Prairie View Senior Living in Tracy, her home for six years until her final illness. An avid lover of animals, Bernie enjoyed the companionship of pets, especially her canaries and dog.

Don't Tell!

I thought of Bernie as my beleaguered big sister. The chapters of her story were written not in ink but in anguish. Bernie was 11 years old when twin sisters joined the Kopriva family. From then on, her life was topsy-turvy.

My memory skipped to June 1, 2022. My niece, Mary, accompanied me on a road trip to visit Bernie at Prairie View Home Healthcare. That was the day she had danced in a wheelchair to the Patsy Cline CD. Music blared down the corridor for all the residents to enjoy. Bernie's health had been sliding down an icy slope for months.

I know in my gut this will be my last visit with my sister!

I put my tears on hold that afternoon. Plastering on a happy face, I laughed and swayed to the country western lyrics.

As evening came, Bernie realized that Mary and I had a long drive ahead of us the next day. The trip was eight hours back to Rapid City.

"You better get going. It will be a tiring day on the road tomorrow," Bernie acknowledged.

How unexpected this thoughtful comment from my sister sounded. Usually, at the end of a visit, she would grumble, "You just got here! Can't you stay longer?"

I had always felt guilty when Bernie complained, like I had failed her once again. The truth was, I was relieved to depart. Our visits were emotionally taxing, often argumentative and draining.

But on that June day, as we readied ourselves to get on the road, I felt only sadness. Bernie's words made me pause.

Is she making it easy for us to go? Does she realize we will not meet again? Is she releasing us?

"Can we pray for you, Bernie?" I asked impulsively.

She eagerly agreed.

No sooner had our prayer ended, than my sister asked, "Can I pray for you for a safe trip home?"

Simultaneously, Mary and I chorused, "Yes!"

Was death listening to our final words, wrapping us in love? Don't cry!

Fewer than seven weeks passed before my foreboding intuition was fulfilled on July 19th. Bernie died in the nearest available hospice house, about 40 miles away.

Many times, I had heard my sister vehemently assert, "I do not want to die in an institution. I want to get a job and be on my own again!"

Death had a mind of its own, with a predestined time and place to claim each one of us. Bernie died on the day of Charles' eighty-second birthday.

Birthdays and death days came and went, like rushing automobiles on a freeway.

Bernie's body was transported to Rapid City for the burial rites. Deacon Larry Kopriva, presided for the wake at Blessed Sacrament Church on August 2. He invited me to give a eulogy. "It doesn't matter how long it is," he stated. Little did he know, the 22 mourners were in for a 37-minute remembrance of someone they had never met.

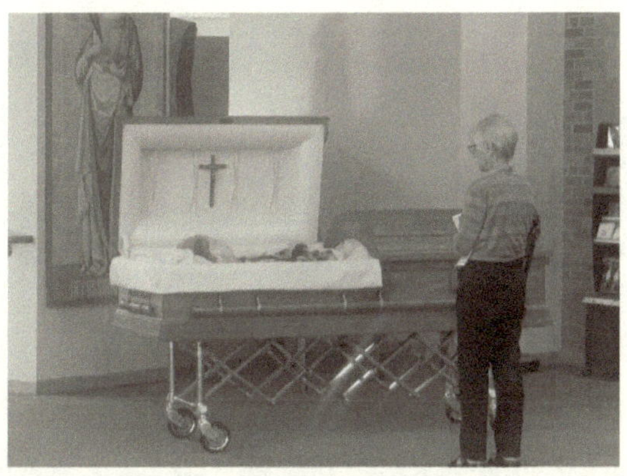

I paused for a quiet moment with my sister before the service began.

At the vigil, I closed my eulogy with a prayer for Bernie and asked that she pray for us. I acknowledged the FaceTime Angel at Prairie View who had helped us to connect during the final weeks of Bernie's life.

Unbeknown to me, my daughter, Carol, made a video of my eulogy for Bernie. When I watched it days later, I felt ashamed that I'd talked for so long! But I felt compelled to tell my nieces and nephews about the Aunt Bernie they never knew.

My brother Greg stood and clapped at the end of the eulogy. We spontaneously hugged one another before I sat down in my seat next to him in the front pew.

The morning following the vigil, Father Tim presided at the funeral liturgy. Since the priest did not know Bernie, Deacon Larry gave the homily in a voice choked with grief. Jim Kopriva and Felix Maes, both nephews, proclaimed Bible passages with voices of sincere faith. Unaccustomed to being honored, Bernie would have been embarrassed by so much attention.

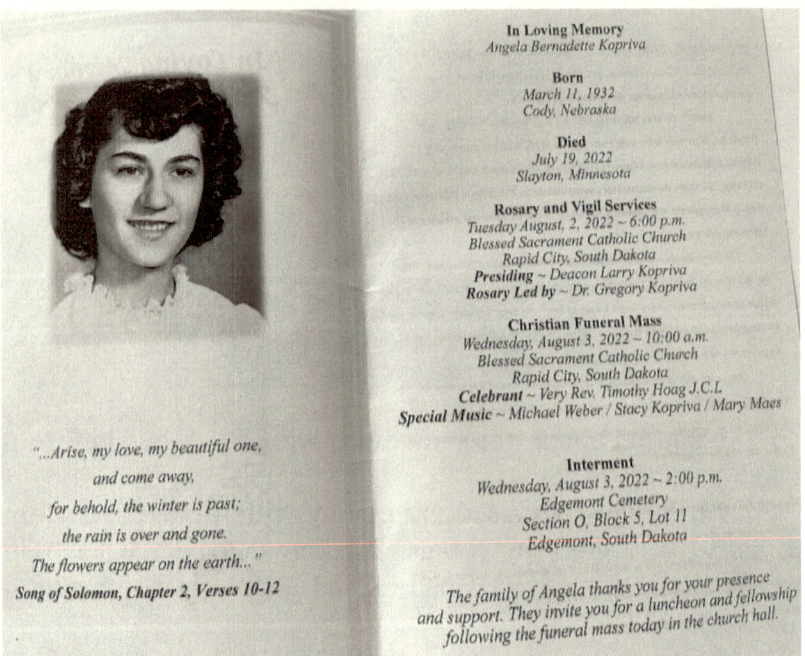

"...Arise, my love, my beautiful one,
and come away,
for behold, the winter is past;
the rain is over and gone.
The flowers appear on the earth..."
Song of Solomon, Chapter 2, Verses 10-12

In Loving Memory
Angela Bernadette Kopriva

Born
March 11, 1932
Cody, Nebraska

Died
July 19, 2022
Slayton, Minnesota

Rosary and Vigil Services
Tuesday August, 2, 2022 ~ 6:00 p.m.
Blessed Sacrament Catholic Church
Rapid City, South Dakota
***Presiding** ~ Deacon Larry Kopriva*
***Rosary Led by** ~ Dr. Gregory Kopriva*

Christian Funeral Mass
Wednesday, August 3, 2022 ~ 10:00 a.m.
Blessed Sacrament Catholic Church
Rapid City, South Dakota
***Celebrant** ~ Very Rev. Timothy Hoag J.C.L*
***Special Music** ~ Michael Weber / Stacy Kopriva / Mary Maes*

Interment
Wednesday, August 3, 2022 ~ 2:00 p.m.
Edgemont Cemetery
Section O, Block 5, Lot 11
Edgemont, South Dakota

The family of Angela thanks you for your presence and support. They invite you for a luncheon and fellowship following the funeral mass today in the church hall.

A luncheon was held in the church basement following Mass. Bernie's memorial video was projected on a screen, while mourners chatted during the meal. Although few had known my sister, friends came to support the Kopriva family, longtime members of Blessed Sacrament.

As lunch ended, I approached Greg urging, "Look at the memorial video showing on the screen! I made it for you."

Greg replied, "Not now. I've got too much going on with Kathryn. I'll watch it later." His wife, Kathryn, 95, had impaired vision. Greg had been her primary caregiver for the past nine years. Greg had remarried a couple years after Rose died.

To the best of my knowledge, Greg never watched Bernie's video. Perhaps he felt too sad. Greg coped by blocking hard times. The same stories I wished to preserve, my brother tried to erase.

I felt lonely.

Was I the only one wanting to tell our story? Did my brother still feel ashamed?

Mass completed, attendants rolled Bernie's closed casket down the central aisle of the church. They hoisted it into the Osheim Schmidt hearse. The vehicle solemnly departed on the 90-mile trip to Edgemont. Cars joined the queue down Highway 79, through the Black Hills, across the flatlands. When everyone arrived at Cemetery Hill, Deacon Larry proceeded with a brief burial liturgy. Family settled under an awning, protected from the blazing August sun.

Greg and I comforted each other at the grave. He gave me the memorial crucifix to hold.

Jim Kopriva piped up, "I have a song to sing for Aunt Bernie. Would that be okay?"

No sooner had we all nodded in astonished consent, he began.

"All My Tears," written by Julie Miller and sung by Emmylou Harris in 1995, stirred us. Jim's solo floated across the prairie like a benediction.

"It don't matter where you bury me. I'll be home, and I'll be free. The wounds this world left on my soul will all be healed, and I'll be whole."

We sat in heavy silence.

Finally, the mortician asked us if we wanted to witness the burial.

We nodded firmly in unison, "Yes."

A pneumatic motor prepared to hoist the coffin into the vault. I noticed, to my disbelief, that Bernie's name, on a ribbon atop the coffin, was misspelled.

"Stop!" I commanded. "Her name is not spelled right!"

"We're all printers here, and we learned early-on to always edit what we print!" Greg remarked impatiently.

An embarrassed assistant hastily appeared with paint to supply the missing letter at the end of Bernadette.

Although appalled at this careless error, we shifted our disgust back to sadness.

Our sister was slowly lowered into the earth that waited to embrace her.

My niece Mary and I returned to Cemetery Hill one year later. Bernie's gravesite was topped with raw earth, just as we had left it. We needed a grave cover for Bernie that would match the graves of Daddy, Mom, and Emilie.

Our plan was to locate a monument company that would mark Bernie's burial spot.

Standing at my family plot I prayed, "God, give peace to my dear ones at last!"

A Gardener's Perspective

A gardener touched life and death whenever she placed her bare hands in the earth. She was familiar with the sacred cycle of beginnings and endings. Dorothy Frances Gurney (1858- 1932) summed up the gift of a garden with a poem.

The kiss of the sun for pardon,
The song of the birds for mirth,
One is nearer God's heart in a garden
Than anywhere else on earth.

A country flower garden, full of bright petals and pleasant scents, captivated viewers. Likewise, a Garden of Stone, moved visitors with its endless rows of tombstones

Memorial Day weekend of 2024 brought the Kopriva clan together at the Edgemont cemetery to ponder and to give thanks. Bernie's grave cover, installed in the Spring of 2024, matched the markers of her parents and little sister, Emilie.

We remembered Rose at the National Guard Cemetery near Sturgis. Gardens of Blossoms and Gardens of Stone brought us to stillness.

Chapter Seventeen
Coming Home

As a 22-year-old woman, just out of undergrad studies at the University of South Dakota in 1965, I stood on the brink of life. Robed with the lightness of adventure and weighed with adult responsibility, I felt exhilarated and afraid. The real world, outside college boundaries, beckoned.

Where am I going to settle down to teach? California, where everyone has a swimming pool, or Colorado, where everyone hikes the Rockies?

Since I loved being outdoors in nature, both locations appealed to me. Of one thing, I was clear. No way would I return to my hometown, Edgemont, South Dakota. Ghosts lurked there, in gray and brown shadows.

Questions had a way of simmering, like a pot of hot soup on the stove. An answer to where I would settle emerged while I was in Missoula, Montana for the summer. I attended the French Institute, sponsored by the National Defense Education Act.

The letter that appeared in my mailbox welcomed me not to California, nor Colorado. Cheyenne, Wyoming had accepted me as a French and English teacher at Carey Junior High.

Since my calendar was teetering on the brink of August, I was eager to get a job nailed down. The offer in Cheyenne was like the proverbial "Bird in the Hand." Wyoming did not have quite the appeal that California or Colorado had. But, at least, it wasn't South Dakota.

Cheyenne is a four-hour bus ride. I won't have to go home often, just for holidays.

Emma K. Lee

A friendly welcome sign belied the sorrow my family had known in our hometown.

Every time I visited my relatives, I found myself heading down Highway 18 and back into a history book of gloom. Strangely, I was attracted to the very ghosts that I wanted to avoid.

During my dutiful trips to see my aging parents, I was drawn to walk streets that saturated me with both nightmares and nostalgia. I discovered I had a love-hate relationship with the little prairie town on the edge of the mountains. Each time I found myself visiting, I thanked God that I had escaped to a new life.

Had I really escaped?

No way!

I recalled the 1961 graduation when I stood on the stage at the Edgemont Armory. My valedictory speech concluded with both sadness and relief. "This will probably be the last time we will all be together. I wish you farewell and fare well!"

I don't want to come here again...but I wish you a happy life.

Despite my urgency to avoid Edgemont, life had its own agenda. Although I desired to run away, I couldn't avoid the call to come back. I kept returning to one particular hilltop beyond the town.

My first connection with Cemetery Hill came from the loss of my infant nephew in February 1961. I was a senior in high school, and death was the last thing I wanted to think about. After a troubled pregnancy, Rose gave birth by caesarean to her third child. RH Factor blood type incompatibility was the culprit that caused the newborn to die at birth.

On a snow-blowing day, Greg, Mom, Daddy, and I laid the innocent baby to rest. The name assigned to him was John Paul, after the current Pope. Greg and Rose were grasping for peace in our Catholic faith as grief tried to swallow them whole. Rose, recovering from surgery, remained in the hospital, unable to attend the funeral.

October 1967, my brothers, Mom, and I gathered on Cemetery Hill once again. We needed to choose a family burial plot. Daddy had just died following a lengthy battle with Parkinson's. Greg decided to purchase six burial sites so that all the family would have a place to be together. Everyone would have a spot except for Greg. He would be buried at the military cemetery near Sturgis, next to Rose.

In a daze, Mom wandered around the cemetery, grieving lost dreams. A troubled marriage of thirty-eight years left her mourning for what might have been.

Mom, I wish I could help you, but I don't know what to say.

Twice in 1992, I was destined to return to Cemetery Hill.

Mom died after years of declining health. I hadn't gone to her deathbed. I assumed her final illness was just one more episode of sporadic maladies. Leaving my son's graduation from the Air Force Academy in 1992 was not what I wanted to do. So, I didn't show up for Mom.

Come on, Mom, just get well. You're always getting sick and feeling better soon. I want to celebrate with my own family right now. I'll visit you when I'm not so busy.

Mom didn't get my message.

She claimed her burial spot next to Daddy within just a few days.

Emilie arrived on the hill only six months later, in December.

Bernie had the next appointment with death in July 2022. She lived to be 90. Once again, the desolate grounds of Cemetery Hill called the family to Edgemont for a burial.

When my niece, Mary, and I visited the Kopriva plot in 2023, I captured pictures of the grassland reserved for Charles and me.

My cemetery spot had been whispering to me, like a friend with open arms. With each family death, I had reluctantly begun to plan my funeral service. I didn't want to burden my children with final arrangements. However, I never completed my first set of plans, begun when the grandkids were toddlers. At that time, I intended the youngsters to give mourners packets of rose petals from my garden.

I didn't die.

The young ones grew up.

Twenty-five years flashed by.

Still, I dragged my feet.

Finally, in 2005, when a diagnosis of thyroid cancer frightened me, I laid out my last will and testament. In 2012, the detection of skin cancer jarred me to make more preparations. Not until 2023, when breast cancer showed up, did I get serious.

Are you coming to Edgemont to claim your burial plot? Can you rest in peace in a place that was anything but peaceful for you?

Much to my surprise, answers came as I gazed across the cemetery skyline.

With the Black Hills and the plateau hovering in the background, I found rest in the land of my birth. From the parting clouds of confusion into the autumn sunlight came assurance.

You were born on the prairie. Return to the prairie when you die.

I knew in an instant that I would come back to Cemetery Hill to stay forever with my family. They had birthed me, formed me, and sent me out into the world.

From dust I had come. I would return to the dust of Cemetery Hill. Accepting my place in the family plot told me that my heart was softening. Grace had brought me to this decision. The prairie grass and the distant mountains proclaimed, like the sign at the city entrance, "Welcome to Edgemont. Welcome home!"

Edgemont was my home. I would stay here forever.

I reached for my journal to safeguard throbbing emotions.

EPIPHANY

A subtle whisper builds to a shocking blast.
Fully awake from slumber amid the ordinary,
I jump as Death grabs for me.
Adrenalin pulsing through my veins, I flee on shaky legs,
while autumn leaves fall languidly to earth.
To a quiet breeze, the wild grass sways.
Distant hills and nearby graves observe knowingly.
Nature calmly dances her patterned steps.
Dare I ignore her eternal song?
Breathe.   Notice.   Cherish.
A mystery, not to be avoided, but honored.
Life and Death are one.
Surrender.
Come home to yourself!

All the world seemed far away and inconsequential from the view on Cemetery Hill. No resistance did I feel, only surrender to the expansive plains that welcomed me. Tossing aside righteous self-determination, I yielded.

I offered myself to the grassland, the warmth of September sun, the assurance of peace. All my days had prepared me for the golden haven of this South Dakota landscape.

Epilogue

No memoir has ever contained all the events of a lifetime. What went into this narrative and what didn't was a deliberate choice that left behind scattered details.

Curious readers have asked, "What about your own kids? Aren't they part of this tale?" The landscape of this story contained the roots of my biologic family tree, not the next-generation branches.

My husband and children were seldom encountered in this drama. They never knew my twin sister. She was locked away in an institution years before their births. However, the ripples of my turbulent childhood spilled over into both my marriage and my parenting.

Not having an example of a stable family to follow, I stumbled my way, seeking tips from self-help books, talk show hosts, and adult education classes. I wanted my kids to have an easier, softer way than I had known. I taught them to be responsible, independent, and hard working because those traits had gotten me through rough times.

In May of 2023, South Dakota Public Broadcasting aired a documentary, "Leaving Redfield". Administrators, caregivers, and former residents shared their firsthand experiences. The transformation of Redfield evolved over decades. Each generation improved upon former conditions and management practices.

The revisioning that occurred at Redfield reflected the broadening social understanding of developmentally delayed folks. They had once been stigmatized as insane or feeble-minded.

Gradually, they emerged as people with potential to contribute to the community. Treatment practices had evolved.

Writing evoked my pain and invited healing. Only by embracing the past, did I find peace rather than vegetating in repression. Every sob escaping my throat had been the refrain of long-held sadness. Every tear I shed washed wounds like gentle ocean waves lapping a sandy shore. Even as my narrative pushed its way to publication, restlessness tugged at me.

This memoir was not a sugar-coated narrative of sweet vignettes. No idyllic Garden of Eden fulfilled all my wishes. Amid the apple trees, snakes continued to slither. Flowers continued to bloom and to fade. Every day mixed light with darkness. Roses had thorns. Such was the reality of life.

Surprising emotions surged when I wrote these chapters. Hazy memories demanded to be revealed. Like an attentive stenographer, I recorded the story in manageable segments. When emotions were high, when I had enough intensity for one day, I closed my computer. I headed to my garden to dig and sweat. Sentiments crushed or uplifted me. Healing has been a gradual process with its own rhythm. Awareness came slowly and unexpectedly.

I grieved for the buried sorrows in my life, like long-neglected children. I chose not to include events too fragile to drag into the spotlight of the public stage. Betrayal of trust is hard to acknowledge and difficult to forgive. Not all stories are to be laid at the feet of prying eyes and curious inquirers.

Just as joy was sometimes unspeakable, so sorrow was, at times, wordless.

The "Don't Tell" commandments, imprinted on me at childhood, have not vanished. In Ecclesiastes 3:7, the Bible differenced a time to speak from a time to be silent. In writing, I have deliberated about what I included and what I didn't.

This memoir is an assortment of random snapshots. Not every picture on the roll of film made its way into the photo album. Powerful scenes, soaked with tears, hit the "cutting floor." I was not ready to tell every secret.

Chapters of this story arose from the storehouse of my unconscious. Stories followed their own sequence, not chronological order. Episodes from distant past mingled with the present, only to flash to the past again. Recollection came with pauses and glides as my memory danced its own jig.

An unexpected diagnosis of breast cancer jerked my focus from the past into the present. Research about treatment options and next-step procedures diverted my attention. At eighty-years-old, I decided to snub traditional medical protocols. Unpredictable side effects seemed costly. Quality of life was more important to me than longevity. I decided to seize each day as it appeared with each sunrise.

End the memoir. Stop the probe into the past. The present is all you have!

My story concluded where it started...with questions. However, not every question required an answer.

I have urged readers to dig deep into their own stories and to feel buried emotions. From Twelve Step recovery, I learned healing came through serving others. Tilling my own garden gave me flowers to share with my neighbors.

Looking back over eight decades, I gradually understood that my family had been my teacher, guiding me to appreciate the miracle each of us is. Peace came from accepting what was...not what might have been. For decades, I regarded Emilie's retardation as a mistake, an accident, a quirk of nature...even my own fault!

The Bible in Second Corinthians 1:3-4 helped me understand that my troubles prepared me to stand compassionately with people in pain. My family of origin readied me for my mission. The only way I could be a credible companion was by facing my hurts and secrets. Writing, counseling and presenting retreats allowed me to pass on the comfort I have received. I have continued to be healed as I help others to heal.

Writing in my journal recently, God gave me a poem...

Emma K. Lee

Psalm of Deliverance
O Child of nightmares, you have run
from the village that imprisoned you.
You fled to the Palisades and to the Rockies,
to lands far away.

In your escaping,
My footfalls vibrated in your ears.
My steady voice directed your path.
While words unspoken pulsed in your throat,
Your grieving heart forgot not lost innocence.
Distance couldn't soothe your aching spirit.

Listen well to what miles and years reveal.
Accept my wisdom within you, not far away.
Slow down. Calm the hurting.
Tenderly caress your fading scars.
Hear my subtle whisperings amid your questionings.
Embrace the unspeakable with gentle hands.

I have protected and guided you.
You did not survive alone or by chance.
Listen to folks pleading for your help.
Give freely what you have received.
Deliverance is not for you alone, but for all.

EKL

Gardener must garden. Writers are destined to write. In accepting what is…not what might have been…we are set free from the past to cherish the present. In life's amazing garden, may all of us find peace amid the brambles and blossoms that line our daily path.

Emma K. Lee
July 23, 2025

End Note: August 2025

The Edgemont High Alumni Association sponsored an all-class reunion during the annual Fall River County Fair. Eager to attend with my walker-bound brothers, I showed up with our clan. Fifteen Koprivas rubbed elbows, including kids and spouses.

Three classmates pulled me aside to chat and share memories.

"My Mom wanted me to be just like you!"

"Kids treated me like an outsider because I lived on a ranch, but you were nice to me."

"You were really smart."

Hearing these surprising comments from my peers gave me a new perspective on myself. At last, I felt like I belonged to this crowd. I was no longer an outsider. These old-timers were my family!

Our Edgemont gathering ended with a trek to Cemetery Hill.

Who will claim the next burial spot?

As we stood at the family plot, I gave my children some funeral instructions.

"I want rose quartz to mark my grave…no ordinary cement cover!"

My brothers and I were home at last.

Author's Notes

A Twelve-Step sponsor, one who had personally walked the walk of addiction, had offered me an unshakeable testimony. Stumbling, falling, and getting up to start over was the pattern of recovery. Embracing powerlessness, releasing shame, disclosing secrets, that was the way to become whole. To help others, I first had to dig deep into my own soil.

Believers from diverse faith communities have inspired me to explore my life and to surrender my expectations of what might have been.

Buddhist teacher Pema Chodron wrote, "Only when we know our own darkness well can we be present with the darkness of others. Compassion becomes real when we recognize our shared humanity."

Anne Morrow Lindbergh, author of Gift from the Sea, wrote "When one is a stranger to oneself, then one is estranged from others, too. If one is out of touch with oneself, then one cannot touch others."

Sadness saturated me when I thought about the tragedy of the Charles Lindbergh Family. In 1932, their first-born was kidnapped from his crib at night. The body of the toddler was discovered weeks later, five miles from home. His skull had been crushed, his body battered. Anne Lindberg's wisdom, born of suffering, inspired me to claim my strength tempered by hardship.

"In the depths of every wound we have survived is the strength we need to live," stated Rachel Naomi Remen, M.D, counselor to terminally ill patients and national bestselling author of My Grandfather's Blessings. Pain was the sharp edge of the surgeon's scalpel which created an open wound, allowing for healthy tissue to grow. I was no longer ashamed of the mental disabilities in my family.

Jeanne Safer, Ph.D. authored *The Normal One: Life with a Difficult or Damaged Sibling.* She elaborated on four symptoms which characterize children having a disabled sibling: premature maturity, survivor guilt, compulsion to achieve, fear of contagion. Her personal and professional insights confirmed my own experience.

As a family therapist, I recognized what had eluded me in childhood. Little kids blamed themselves when parents fought, divorced, or died. Self-blame was a coping mechanism whenever family life was out of control. My self-judgement had not been based on culpability, but on trying to comprehend tragedy. It was easier for me to believe I caused problems than to accept suffering without reason. Guilt was more manageable than helplessness.

My memoir has not focused on preaching a sermon on how people should live. Nor has it been a professional case study with tools for emotional healing.

My intention has been to help readers embrace their questions, acknowledge pain, and release expectations. As a family therapist, a spiritual director, and an adult catechist, I have had a front-row seat to courage. I companioned folks who discovered strength as they crawled through the mud of affliction.

After the terrorist attacks on the Twin Towers in New York on September 11, 2001, I witnessed a notable increase in faith conversions. Adult baptisms reached a higher record than at any other time in my 27 years of parish service. Pain either caused people to turn from God or to go deeper inside themselves to find God.

Many distanced from God during hard times. I, too, had been a doubter, expecting life to follow my plan. Yet, I was true to myself and to God when I examined life through a microscope. Journaling and gardening helped sort out my confusion. Adversity had been the seed of my growth that prepared me to stand with folks amid weeds and rocks.

In 1902, the German poet Rainier Maria Rilke wrote *Letters to a Young Poet*. His words have profoundly encouraged me.

"Be patient toward all that is unresolved in your heart and try to love the questions themselves like locked rooms and like books that are written in a very foreign tongue. Do not seek the answers, which cannot be given to you now because you would not be able to live them. And the point is to live everything. Live the questions now. Perhaps you will then gradually, without noticing it, live your way into the answer, one distant day in the future."

A Gardener's Perspective

Gardeners love to put their hands and their hoes in the soil. Raking, plowing, and digging in the earth is as natural as breathing. The pause between inhaling and exhaling mirrors the gap when a dormant seed waits to sprout.

In Colorado, a hot summer afternoon can vanish overnight, bringing a temperature drop of 40 degrees the next day. The wall calendar and the weather reporter predict changes. Control of the climate does not rest with the one who plants seeds nor the one who foretells the arrival of daybreak.

Clay, hard as a stone, and sand permeable as a cloud, claim territory on the landscape. Gardeners need a sturdy shovel to dig. Some seeds require depth, others shallow graves in which to germinate.

The gardener, absorbed in nurturing unseen growth, waters, fertilizes, and weeds. Seasons of rain and draught come and go surreptitiously. Hours of vigorous work pass as quickly as vanishing thoughts. The growth or death of plants is beyond the gardener's control. Survival and fecundity rest with the Master Gardener.

Not all folks are made to garden. People chosen for the privilege of tending the earth dig with vigor. They do not own the soil. Plants blossom and fade. . .some never reach harvest. The planter does not control the crop's destiny. Tending the soil requires working, waiting, and releasing the outcome.

Truth be told, it is the garden that grows the gardener. The earth is a teacher. The gardener is a learner. Accepting the results of a harvest as though the planter had personally selected that crop, is a challenge. Surrender to the Creator requires daily intention.

My twin sister, Emilie, was an innocent seed who grew in the Kopriva garden. She emerged slowly, quietly, resting in the present. . .unbound by past and future. The Master Gardener appointed her as a guardian angel to watch over her family throughout every passing season.

／
Acknowledgements

A memoir, like a country flower garden, needs support to make it bloom. My thanks extend to many who spurred me on to bring this story from the root cellar of buried secrets to the sunshine of the printed page.

Encouragement from my family kept me digging deep into the past. James Lee, my son, and my grandkids found no shame in a story about developmental delay and mental illness. Millie, Lauchlan and Quinn Bramschreiber joined Raina and Ellie Lee, and Cecilia Truitt, to affirm folks on the fringes of normalcy. I am grateful to my daughter, Carol Bramschreiber, and to my grandson, Jack Lee, who patiently guided me through technical snafus with my computer. My brothers, Gregory Kopriva, DDS and Charles Kopriva, MD joined me in delving into childhood scenes that evoked both chuckles and sobs. Special thanks go to Deacon Larry Kopriva and Mary Maes who shared their spiritual road map as well as their footsteps through our family stomping grounds.

Jungian therapists and spiritual directors, Betsy Caprio and Tom Hedberg taught me to honor my nightmares and to return home as many times as I needed to explore the skeletons in my closet.

I owe a shout-out to writers who read my story and nudged me to keep going: Rich Egan, Dick Sunstrom, Bill Walker, Terry Robinson, Marietta Montaine, Sonja Wright, Doctor Trajn Boughan, Darlice Johnson Dockter, Marsha Smith, Hugh Burns, Peg Monahan Shannon, Michele Deslauriers, Kathy Broghammer, Sister Marlou Ricke, and Sister Theresa O'Grady, OSB.

Adult Children of Alcoholics taught me that we are as sick as our secrets. I'm grateful to Patrick Carnes Ph. D. who gave me a clear lens to review my life. I highly recommend A Gentle Path Through the Twelve Steps: The Classic Guide for all People in the Process of Recovery.

Along with punctuation and grammar tips, my publication editor, Suzanne Holland, M.S. inspired me with her expertise from teaching folks living with developmental delays.

German Catholic theologian and philosopher Meister Eckhart, who died in 1328, advised, "If the only prayer you ever say in your whole life is 'Thank you', that would be enough." To all who encouraged me to bring this memoir to life, I send my humble prayer of gratitude.

Thank you.

About the Author

Emma Lee is a retired Licensed Marriage and Family Therapist. She has served in church ministry for forty-five years as a teacher, bereavement counselor, retreat leader, and spiritual director. The passion of her life is guiding travelers through gentle showers and startling thunderstorms, integrating spiritual growth and psychological health. An avid gardener and an ardent journal-keeper, Emma enjoys digging deep with the trowel of memory into the rich soil of the past, uncovering an intriguing assortment of brambles and blossoms. Each chapter of this narrative ends with "A Gardener's Perspective" which entwines family transitions and changing seasons.

www.ingramcontent.com/pod-product-compliance
Lightning Source LLC
LaVergne TN
LVHW091146080826
845145LV00008B/2270

9781940025711